BORDERLINE PERSONALITY DISORDER

A COMPLETE BPD GUIDE FOR
MANAGING YOUR EMOTIONS AND
IMPROVING YOUR RELATIONSHIPS

JUDY DYER

BORDERLINE PERSONALITY DISORDER:
A Complete BPD Guide for Managing Your Emotions and
Improving Your Relationships
by Judy Dyer

ISBN: 978-1989588475

ALSO BY JUDY DYER

CONTENTS

INTRODUCTION

A t the time of writing this book, 1.6% of the population meets the criteria for borderline personality disorder, or BPD.[i] There's a good chance you will meet someone with the condition at some point—assuming that you haven't already.

BPD is a misunderstood mental illness. People with this diagnosis are often stereotyped as manipulative or crazy. This stigma stops them from seeking help and leaves them feeling alienated from family and friends. This book separates the myths from the facts. It is a straightforward guide to the symptoms, causes, and treatment of BPD and contains practical advice as well about seeking help and living with the condition.

BPD is also known as emotionally unstable personality disorder (EUPD). For the sake of consistency, the condition is referred to as BPD throughout this book, but you might hear both terms if you work with a mental health professional or read about BPD elsewhere.

If you think you might have BPD, this guide will help you decide whether it's time to seek professional help. Perhaps you've read a few articles about BPD and suspect you have some or all of the symptoms. Maybe you're scared or anxious about what getting a BPD diagnosis would mean for you. In these pages, you'll learn more about what you can expect when you reach out to a doctor or therapist.

You will also discover self-help strategies that empower you to deal with your emotions. If you have BPD, you probably cycle through lots of different feelings. Throughout this book, you'll learn how to take back control through self-help, psychotherapy, and medication. With proper treatment, it's possible to make a full recovery.[ii]

Maybe you haven't picked up this book because you have symptoms of BPD. Perhaps you know or suspect that someone you're close to has the condition. If you have a friend, relative, colleague, or partner with BPD, this guide will help you support them. BPD is a lonely illness; it can be hard to explain to other people how it feels to live with the condition. Reading up on the topic will give you valuable insight.

The first step is to understand exactly what it means to have BPD. In the next chapter, we'll take a close look at the signs and symptoms to watch out for.

JOIN OUR SUPPORT GROUP

In order to maximize the value you receive from this book, I highly encourage you to join our tight-knit community on Facebook. Here you will be able to connect and share strategies with others dealing with BPD in order to continue your growth.

Taking this journey alone is not recommended, and this can be an excellent support network for you.

It would be great to connect with you there,

Judy Dyer

To Join, Visit:

www.pristinepublish.com/empathgroup

DOWNLOAD THE AUDIO VERSION OF THIS BOOK FREE

If you love listening to audiobooks on the go or would enjoy a narration as you read along, I have great news for you. You can download the audio book version of *BPD* for FREE (Regularly $14.95) just by signing up for a FREE 30-day audible trial!

Visit: www.pristinepublish.com/audiobooks

YOUR FREE GIFT - HEYOKA EMPATH

A lot of empaths feel trapped, as if they've hit a glass ceiling they can't penetrate. They know there's another level to their gift, but they can't seem to figure out what it is. They've read dozens of books, been to counselling, and confided in other experienced empaths, but that glass ceiling remains. They feel alone, and alienated from the rest of the world because they know they've got so much more to give, but can't access it. Does this sound like you?

The inability to connect to your true and authentic self is a tragedy. Being robbed of the joy of embracing the full extent of your humanity is a terrible misfortune. The driving force of human nature is to live according to one's own sense of self, values, and emotions. Since the beginning of time, philosophers, writers, and scholars have argued that authenticity is one of the most important elements of an individual's well-being.

When there's a disconnect between a person's inner being and their expressions, it can be psychologically damaging. Heyokas are the most powerful type of empaths, and many of them are not fully aware of who they are. While other empaths experience feelings of overwhelm and exhaustion from absorbing others' energy and emotions, heyoka empaths experience an additional aspect of exhaustion in that they are fighting a constant battle with their inability to be completely authentic.

The good news is that the only thing stopping you from becoming your authentic self is a lack of knowledge. You need to know exactly who you are so you can tap into the resources that have been lying dormant within you. In this bonus e-book, you'll gain in-depth information about the seven signs that you're a heyoka empath, and why certain related abilities are such powerful traits. You'll find many of the answers to the questions you've been searching for your entire life such as:

- Why you feel uncomfortable when you're around certain people
- How you always seem to find yourself on the right path even though your decisions are not based on logic or rationale
- The reason you get so offended when you find out others have lied to you
- Why you analyze everything in such detail
- The reason why humor is such an important part of your life
- Why you refuse to follow the crowd, regardless of the consequences
- The reason why strangers and animals are drawn to you

There are three main components to authenticity: understanding who you are, expressing who you are, and letting the world experience who you are. Your first step on this journey is to know who you are, and with these seven signs that you're a heyoka empath, you'll find out. I've included snippets about the first three signs in this description to give you full confidence that you're on the right track:

Sign 1: You Feel and Understand Energy

Heyoka empaths possess a natural ability to tap into energy. They can walk into a room and immediately discern the atmosphere. When an individual walks past them, they can literally see into their soul because they can sense the aura that person is carrying. But empaths also understand their own energy, and they allow it to guide them. You will often hear this ability referred to as "the sixth sense." The general consensus is that only a few people have this gift. But the reality is that everyone was born with the ability to feel energy; it's just been demonized and turned into something spooky, when in actual fact, it's the most natural state to operate in.

Sign 2: You are Led by Your Intuition

Do you find that you just know things? You don't spend hours, days, and weeks agonizing over decisions, you can just feel that something is the right thing to do, and you go ahead and do it. That's because you're led by your intuition and you're connected to the deepest part of yourself. You know your soul, you listen to it, and you trust it. People like Oprah Winfrey, Steve Jobs and Richard Branson followed their intuition steadfastly and it led them to become some of the most successful people in the history of the world. Living from within is the way we were created to be, and those who trust this ability will find their footing in life a lot more quickly than others. Think of it as a GPS system: when it's been programmed properly, it will always take you to your destination via the fastest route.

Sign 3: You Believe in Complete Honesty

In general, empaths don't like being around negative energy, and there's nothing that can shift a positive frequency faster than dishonesty. Anything that isn't the truth is a lie, even the tiny ones that we excuse away as "white lies." And as soon as they're released from someone's mouth, so is negative energy. Living an authentic life requires complete honesty at all times, and although the truth may hurt, it's better than not being able to trust someone. Heyoka empaths get very uncomfortable in the presence of liars. They are fully aware that the vibrations of the person don't match the words they are saying. Have you ever experienced a brain freeze mid-conversation? All of a sudden you just couldn't think straight, you couldn't articulate yourself properly, and things just got really awkward? That's because your empath antenna picked up on a lie.

Heyoka Empath: 7 Signs You're A Heyoka Empath & Why It's So Powerful is a revolutionary tool that will help you transition from uncertainty to complete confidence in who you are. In this easy-to-read guide, I will walk you through exactly what makes you a heyoka empath. I've done the research for you, so no more spending hours, days, weeks, and even years searching for answers, because everything you need is right here in this book.

You have a deep need to share yourself with the world, but you've been too afraid because you knew something was missing. The information within the pages of this book is the missing piece in the jigsaw puzzle of your life. There's no turning back now!

Get *Heyoka Empath* for Free by Visiting

www.pristinepublish.com/empathbonus

CHAPTER 1:

WHAT IS BPD?

Everyone with BPD has a unique set of experiences. For example, some people have trouble keeping their temper under control. For others, feelings of emptiness are the worst part of their illness.

WHAT IS A PERSONALITY DISORDER?

Your personality is made up of your behaviors, thoughts, and feelings. Taken together, they set you apart from others and make you unique.

There's no such thing as a "best" personality type. You might be optimistic or cynical, outspoken or quiet, easy-going or highly organized. We are all different, and that's OK. As long as your personality doesn't stop you from living a fulfilling life or forming relationships, there's no reason to worry. However, some people have personality traits that make it hard for them to function in everyday life. Mental health professionals say that someone with this problem has a personality disorder.

A personality disorder is a set of unhelpful, destructive behaviors and traits that persist over time and in different situations. These disorders usually start in adolescence. By adulthood, someone with a personality disorder routinely uses unhealthy behaviors and coping strategies, and this causes problems at college, work, and at home.

Exercise: How Would You Describe Your Personality?

Write a list of at least 10 traits that you feel describes your personality. Are these traits positive, neutral, or negative?

SIGNS YOU MAY HAVE A PERSONALITY DISORDER[iii]

Consider whether any of the following apply to you:

1. **You fell into patterns of unhelpful thinking and behavior as a child or teenager, and you're still using them as an adult.**
   For example, you may always assume that people think the worst of you or that no one can be trusted.

2. **Your feelings, behaviors, and thoughts make it hard for you to function in daily life.**
   For instance, if you find it difficult to keep your temper under control, you might spend a lot of time feeling so angry that you're distracted from your work or studies.

3. **Your problems affect your relationships, work, studies, hobbies, and friendships.**
   Personality disorders are stable across different situations. Some people have specific triggers that make their symptoms worse, such as starting a romantic relationship or managing a heavy workload, but personality disorders usually affect all areas of a person's life.

4. **Your problems aren't caused by another medical condition or by substance abuse.**

   Head injuries, alcohol dependency, and other psychiatric conditions can cause symptoms that are similar to BPD, so these have to be ruled out before you are given a diagnosis.

SYMPTOMS OF BPD

The main hallmarks of BPD are unstable moods, unstable relationships, and unstable self-image.

In the US, there are nine criteria mental health professionals use when deciding whether someone has BPD. To get a diagnosis, you have to meet five of them.[iv]

1. **You have a strong fear of being abandoned that affects your behavior.**

   For example, if your partner has gone away for a work trip, you might call them excessively and worry that they are cheating on you, even if you have no evidence of that or any reason to distrust them.

2. **You have intense moods and emotions, and they can change fast.**

   For example, you may feel very sad for a few hours and then suddenly feel confident and happy for no apparent reason. Some people have several mood swings per day; others have a few per week.

3. **Your relationships are unstable and intense.**

   To you, people are often "good" or "bad" with nothing in between. Some medical professionals use the terms "black and white thinking" or "all or nothing thinking" to describe this phenomenon. Another popular term is "splitting."

People with BPD tend to idealize people and overlook their faults—that is until the person makes a mistake. Of course, because there is no such thing as a perfect person, this is bound to happen sooner or later. Someone with BPD may go back and forth, casting someone in the role of an angel one day and a demon the next.

4. **You have a poorly defined sense of self.**
   You might not know exactly who you are, and your identity may change depending on who you're with. Your interests and goals change frequently. For example, one day you might want to go to medical school, and a week later you might feel determined to become a stay-at-home parent instead.

5. **You feel empty much of the time, despite your capacity for intense emotions.**
   You may have a general sense of not knowing what your purpose in life is. Everything may seem pointless. One minute you may be numb; the next, overwhelmed by sadness or happiness.

6. **You feel compelled to act on destructive impulses.**
   You might binge eat, take drugs, spend too much money on things you don't need, drive too fast, or have sex with people you hardly know.

7. **You experience dissociation, paranoia, or both when you're under intense stress.**
   We all dissociate sometimes. If you have ever become lost in a book and suddenly realized hours have passed while

you were reading, or if you've ever driven somewhere and arrived at your destination with no recollection of your route, you have experienced dissociation. While dissociating, you may feel as though you're watching your body or the world around you from a distance. This is a very common symptom of BPD; only 24% of people with BPD report that they have no dissociative experiences.[v]

During paranoid episodes, you might feel as though no one can be trusted, even your close friends, partner, or relatives. You may assume that everyone is out to take advantage of you, or that they are plotting to harm you. For example, if a work colleague makes a snide remark, you might interpret it as the start of an organized campaign of harassment. Paranoid thoughts occur on a spectrum. Your thoughts might be mild, all-consuming, or somewhere in between.

8. **You have regular bouts of strong anger that are difficult to control.**
    Everyone gets angry sometimes. But if you often find yourself overreacting to minor setbacks or insults, it could be a sign of BPD. People with BPD take longer than other people to calm down when they're upset or annoyed. This can put a strain on relationships because good communication is a real challenge when you are hypersensitive to criticism.

9. **You think about suicide, want to commit suicide, or harm yourself.**
    Approximately 75% of people with BPD attempt to end their lives at least once and 10% will die by suicide.[vi] If you are thinking about harming yourself, you must take

these thoughts seriously. In Chapter 12, you will learn how to handle suicidal urges and behavior. It's common for people with BPD to harm themselves or engage in impulsive, destructive behaviors after drinking alcohol or abusing illegal substances.[vii]

These criteria are from the Diagnostic and Statistical Manual of Mental Disorders (DSM), which is known as the "bible of psychiatry" in the US. Now in its 5th edition, it is published by the American Psychiatric Association. Psychiatrists, social workers, and other mental health professionals use the DSM to decide whether someone has a mental health condition.

Exercise: Do You Recognize BPD Symptoms In Yourself?

Reread the symptom list above. Although you cannot diagnose yourself with a mental illness, there's a chance you have BPD if you can relate to at least five items on the list. Which symptoms affect you the most, and why? Make some notes; these will be useful later if you see a doctor or therapist.

How Do People with BPD Behave?

No two people with BPD are identical, but there are experiences and behaviors that seem to occur in a large number of patients.

1. **They change their life plans on a frequent basis.**
    If you have an unstable sense of self, you might not know what kind of career, relationship, or lifestyle would suit you best. As a result, you may flit from one potential idea to another, never settling on a path. As the years go by,

you might feel as though you've wasted your potential. (Note, however, that people carve out new paths at all ages. It's not too late to pursue your dreams.)

2. **They fail to achieve their goals.**

Major goals, such as completing a degree, become difficult or impossible if you have to deal with erratic moods and identity disturbances. Some people with BPD believe themselves to be "bad" people who don't deserve to succeed. As a result, they fall into a pattern of self-sabotage. Over time, as they continue to miss their goals, they come to view themselves as people who will never make progress. Eventually, they may stop trying to improve their lives.

3. **They schedule lots of activities to avoid feeling alone.**

Fear of being alone or terror at the thought of being abandoned can drive someone with BPD to fill their days and evenings with social activities and dates. An active social life is healthy, but using others as a distraction is not.

4. **They stay in abusive or harmful relationships to avoid being single.**

For those afraid of breaking up with someone, staying with a toxic or abusive partner can seem preferable to being alone. Some people with BPD can leave bad relationships, but they need to have another set up before they break up with their partner. They may have a pattern of overlapping relationships that are unusually dramatic and unstable.

5. **They use drugs or alcohol to manage their feelings.**
   Drinking and taking drugs can be an effective short-term antidepressant or mood booster, but substance abuse is not a viable long-term coping strategy. If you develop a dependency or addiction, you have to contend with another problem on top of your BPD symptoms. Drugs and alcohol also increase the risk of impulsive behavior.

6. **They get into financial difficulties.**
   Retail therapy can be a short-term distraction from overwhelming feelings, and shopping can become an addiction. Gambling is another risky, impulse-driven behavior that can land someone in debt.

   Lots of people with personality disorders are partially or wholly dependent on government social services or public assistance. BPD symptoms make it hard to find and keep a job, and they put a strain on professional relationships.[viii]

7. **They seek medical help more often than the general population.**
   Although only 1.6% of the population has BPD, 6.4% of primary care patients meet the criteria.[ix] This means that people with BPD visit doctors far more often than most people. They are more likely to suffer from a range of ailments, including diabetes, obesity, osteoarthritis, headaches, fibromyalgia, and lower back pain. They are more likely than the general population to smoke, drink too much alcohol, and get too little exercise.[x]

ARE THERE DIFFERENT TYPES OF BPD?

As you learned earlier in this chapter, there are nine BPD symptoms in the DSM, and you must show five of them to qualify for a diagnosis. This means there are 256 possible combinations that meet the criteria.[xi] At the moment, the DSM-5—the most popular psychiatric manual in the US—does not describe BPD subtypes.

This book deals mainly with BPD as described in the DSM, but it's a good idea to familiarize yourself with another system used in other parts of the world: the International Classification of Diseases (ICD-10) manual. If your doctor has diagnosed you using this system rather than the DSM, they will use the term "emotionally unstable personality disorder" (EUPD) rather than BPD. They will also tell you whether your EUPD is "impulsive" or "borderline."[xii]

If you have the **impulsive subtype,** you are likely to struggle with regulating your behavior, keeping your temper under control, and responding appropriately to criticism. People with this subtype often have anger management problems.

If you are diagnosed with the **borderline subtype,** you are likely to struggle with a shifting sense of identity, to have intense and unstable relationships, and to suffer feelings of chronic emptiness. Self-harm, suicide threats, and completed suicide are more frequent in people with this subtype.

The mental health community hasn't yet come to any agreement on what treatments work best for BPD or EUPD subtypes. Whether you are told you have BPD, impulsive EUPD, or borderline EUPD, you are likely to be offered the same kinds of therapy outlined later in this book.

WHAT IS "QUIET BPD"?

When people talk about "quiet BPD," they are referring to BPD symptoms that aren't obvious to anyone other than the sufferer. Those with so-called quiet BPD "act in" rather than act out. They turn all their negative feelings inward and don't usually lash out at, or argue with, other people. To the outside world, someone with quiet BPD may appear "normal." They appear high-functioning, try to please other people, and hide their emotions.[xiii]

Quiet BPD can be a useful term for some people who don't experience dramatic BPD symptoms such as self-harm or angry outbursts. However, this term has no official meaning, and it isn't widely used in medicine. It isn't included in the DSM or the ICD-10 criteria, and it isn't used anywhere else in this book.

MYTHS ABOUT BPD

1. **BPD only affects women.**
    It's true that most people diagnosed with BPD are female. Women make up 66%-75% of the BPD population.[xiv] But many men also have this condition. Men are often more reluctant to seek help for mental health problems, so the real percentage of male sufferers could be much higher than the statistics suggest.

2. **PD only affects young people.**
    BPD symptoms tend to appear in adolescence and early adulthood. However, the condition does not suddenly disappear in a person's 30s, 40s, or beyond.[xv]

3. **You can never recover from BPD.**
    For most people, BPD symptoms improve. Research shows that 15 years after diagnosis, 75% of BPD patients

no longer meet the diagnostic criteria. After 27 years, this figure rises to 92%.[xvi] Another study with 290 BPD patients found that 16 years following diagnosis, 99% had been in remission for at least two years, and 78% had been in remission for at least eight.[xvii]

Some people find that their symptoms come and go. They may enter a period of remission, but then relapse. Yet the numbers offer hope. A typical BPD sufferer can expect to feel better with time.

4. People with BPD are manipulative.

BPD is an illness that has a distinctive set of symptoms. People with the condition may behave in a way that seems irrational or attention-seeking, but they are no more manipulative than the rest of the population. Self-injury, emotional outbursts, and suicide attempts are usually an expression of psychological pain rather than a means of exploiting or controlling other people.[xviii]

5. People with BPD are violent and dangerous.

There is no evidence that having a diagnosis of BPD is a risk factor for violent behavior in the general population.[xix]

6. BPD is rare.

This myth holds a grain of truth. BPD affects 1.6% of the population, so it's relatively uncommon. However, 15-28% of people admitted to psychiatric treatment in hospitals have BPD.

7. BPD is impossible to treat.

Until recently, BPD was considered difficult to treat. The good news is that there are several evidence-based therapies available that we know work well for people with BPD. We'll go into greater detail about treatment options later in the book. It is entirely possible to live a fulfilling life with BPD, even if your symptoms have been severe.[xx]

You need to find a clinician who is well trained in treating your condition. This is because the relationship between a BPD patient and their doctor or therapist is a big factor in how well the treatment works.

Exercise: What Did You Know About BPD?

Before picking up this book, what did you know about BPD? Did you believe any of the myths above? If so, why?

SUMMARY

- BPD is a personality disorder. Personality disorders are unhelpful, destructive ways of thinking about and relating to yourself, others, and the world around you.
- Personality disorders show up early in life. The symptoms start in adolescence.
- There are nine diagnostic criteria mental health professionals use when diagnosing BPD. They include fear of abandonment, feelings of emptiness, and impulsive behaviors.
- BPD is associated with other medical problems, substance abuse, and financial instability.
- There are lots of myths out there about BPD, so it's important to educate yourself and, if possible, your loved ones about the condition.

CHAPTER 2:

DIAGNOSING BPD

The first step in getting help for BPD is to get an accurate diagnosis. Research shows that some therapies are much more helpful for BPD than others, so knowing whether you or your loved one has the condition will set you on the right track when it comes to choosing a treatment.

WHO CAN DIAGNOSE BPD?

You might see one or more of the following if you're being assessed for BPD:

Psychiatrists are medical doctors who specialize in the diagnosis and treatment of mental illness. They can prescribe medication and may also offer talk-based treatments (psychotherapy). Psychiatrists tend to treat the most severe forms of mental illness, including severe depression and schizophrenia.

Clinical psychologists receive extensive training in human behavior and mental illnesses. They normally hold a Ph.D. in psychology. They can diagnose mental illnesses and provide psychotherapy but cannot prescribe medication. Psychologists tend to work with clients over a longer period of time compared with psychiatrists.

Although they are knowledgeable about mental illnesses, they do not have medical training. If they know or suspect that someone has a physical illness alongside psychological problems, they will often work with a psychiatrist to ensure the person gets the best possible care.

General Practitioners (GP) can diagnose mental health problems. They usually diagnose and treat mild mental illness. However, because they are not specialists in this area, they tend to refer patients with moderate to severe symptoms to a psychiatrist for a comprehensive assessment.

Licensed Clinical Social Workers (LCSW) are trained in assessing, diagnosing, and treating mental illness. They are licensed to practice individual, family, and group therapy. They cannot prescribe medication and have no medical training.

Psychiatric Mental Health Advanced Practice Registered Nurses (PMH-APRN) diagnose and treat psychiatric difficulties. They hold postgraduate qualifications in mental health nursing and are authorized to prescribe medication. They can also use psychotherapy in the treatment of mental health problems.

WHAT HAPPENS DURING THE DIAGNOSTIC PROCESS?

During a clinical interview, a mental health professional asks their patient about their symptoms. They will ask about the patient's relationships, whether they are functioning at work or school, whether they experience mood swings, unusual thoughts, or any other psychiatric symptoms such as hallucinations or paranoia. This kind of interview should be thorough and can last over an hour. Sometimes, a mental health professional might want to see a patient several times before they feel comfortable making a formal diagnosis.

It's easy to mistake BPD for another medical condition, so it's vital to gain as much background information as possible. When you go for an evaluation, your provider will want to rule out other conditions that can cause similar symptoms to BPD, including:

Bipolar disorder: Mood swings and relationship difficulties are common in both BPD and bipolar disorder. The key difference is that in BPD, mood swings are more frequent and are often triggered by relationship problems. In bipolar disorder, episodes of depression and mania typically last weeks or even months, whereas BPD episodes usually last hours or a couple of days.[xxi] People with BPD also experience more guilt and shame than people with either bipolar disorder or depression.[xxii]

Post-traumatic stress disorder (PTSD): Along with flashbacks and nightmares, people with PTSD often show typical BPD symptoms, including mood swings, substance abuse, and inappropriate feelings of guilt.[xxiii]

Schizophrenia: Some people with BPD have episodes of paranoia or other psychotic symptoms, such as hallucinations. Because these are common symptoms among people diagnosed with schizophrenia, mental health professionals may conclude that someone who initially appeared to have BPD actually has schizophrenia instead.

Alcohol and substance abuse disorders: Drugs and alcohol can trigger mood swings, damage relationships, and lead to impulsive or reckless behavior.

Other personality disorders: People with histrionic or narcissistic personality disorders sometimes behave in a similar way to people with BPD. For example, people with histrionic tendencies often act in an outlandish way that can make normal relationships hard to sustain.

BPD OFTEN CO-EXISTS WITH OTHER CONDITIONS

Most (85%) of people with BPD have at least one other mental health condition. Depression is the most common; over 50% of BPD patients meet the criteria.[xxiv] Almost 9 in 10 (88%) have an anxiety disorder, 47-56% have PTSD, and 50-65% abuse alcohol or drugs.[xxv] This is called "co-morbidity."

Making the right diagnosis requires time and skill. Waiting for a diagnosis can be frustrating, but a good provider will want to make sure they've built up a clear picture of your situation and history before diagnosing you.

HOW TO TALK TO YOUR DOCTOR

Making an appointment to talk to a professional about your symptoms is a big step. It's normal to feel worried, relieved, or both at the thought of telling your doctor how you feel.

If you are seeing a primary care physician (GP), see if you can find one that has a special interest in mental health matters. They should be sympathetic to your concerns.

Here are some tips to make the process less overwhelming:

1. **Go in with realistic expectations.**
   Even the best doctor in the world can't make you feel better right away. If you have BPD, it's unlikely you will get a diagnosis on the same day. If your GP thinks you

might have BPD or another serious mental health problem, they will refer you to a specialist.

2. **Write down what you want to say.**
   If you think your mind might go blank when you get into the doctor's office, make a few notes on a piece of paper to guide the conversation. Jot down facts about your symptoms, when they started, and the impact they have on your daily life.

3. **Remember that doctors are human, and they don't always have great listening skills.**
   Not all doctors are equally knowledgeable about mental illness. If your doctor brushes you off or doesn't seem to understand what you are saying, seek a second opinion. It's disheartening when a doctor can't or won't help you, but keep trying. You can and will find someone who will listen.

4. **Taking someone with you can help, especially if they have seen how your symptoms affect your life.**
   A trusted friend or relative can also advocate on your behalf if the doctor is unhelpful or rude.

5. **Some doctors don't have a positive view of self-diagnosis, so talk about your symptoms rather than labels.**
   For instance, it is generally better to say, "I have a lot of mood swings that are making it hard for me to form relationships, and I self-harm regularly" rather than "I've been doing some reading lately, and I think I might have Borderline Personality Disorder."

6. **Be honest.**

   If you have BPD, you might have behaved in ways that made you feel ashamed afterward. It's hard to open up about events you'd rather forget. However, it's important that your doctor understands how your symptoms have affected your life. They are there to provide care, not to make moral judgments.

   Some people worry that their doctor will have them sanctioned if they tell the truth about their self-harming behavior or suicidal thoughts. This is very unlikely to happen. Although laws vary by country, as a general rule, you will be detained in a hospital only if you pose a significant risk to yourself or others or if there is no other way you can get the treatment you need.

   Most mental health professionals much prefer to treat patients in the community, or at least arrange for voluntary hospitalization, which is much less restrictive than forcible detention. There are lots of treatment options that don't require a hospital stay, such as medication, talking therapies, and outpatient programs. We'll take a closer look at treatments for BPD later in the book.

7. **Plan a reward.**

   Give yourself something to look forward to after your appointment. You could go see a movie, get premium coffee, or buy yourself a small gift.

8. **Remember that you are not alone.**

   General practitioners see people with mental health problems every day. They may not be experts on BPD, but they will have helped many other patients in your position.

SUMMARY

- Getting the right diagnosis is key because it ensures you get the most suitable treatment.
- Psychiatrists, GPs, and other health and social care professionals can diagnose you with BPD.
- You will be asked a lot of questions about your symptoms and medical history.
- You may have to undergo more than one interview before receiving a formal diagnosis.
- Telling a doctor about your symptoms takes courage, but you can make it easier for yourself by preparing well for your appointment.

CHAPTER 3:

WHAT CAUSES BPD?

Although we don't know for sure what causes BPD, there's an increasing body of evidence that can help us understand why some people fall into rigid, unhelpful patterns of thinking and behavior. In this chapter, we'll look at the role of genetics, family upbringing, parenting, abuse, and trauma.

CAN YOU INHERIT BPD?

If you have a close relative with BPD, you're more likely to have it too. According to a Swedish population study of over 1.8 million people, BPD is 46% heritable.[xxvi] In a Norwegian study with pairs of twins, the BPD concordance rate was 38% for identical and 11% for non-identical twins. So we know that genetics aren't destiny when it comes to BPD, but they play a significant role.[xxvii]

Note that there's a difference between a "BPD gene" and genes that increase someone's susceptibility to the personality traits and behaviors seen in BPD, such as difficulty in regulating emotions or a tendency to behave impulsively. There is no single gene that triggers BPD.

IS THERE A LINK BETWEEN PARENTING STYLE AND BPD?

There is no such thing as a perfect parent, but there is a basic standard of parenting that a mother or father needs to meet if their child is to grow up into a psychologically healthy adult. Ideally, a mother or father will teach their child that it's normal and OK to feel and express emotions. Unfortunately, some parents won't or cannot do this. As a result, their children grow up unable to manage their own feelings.

There is a reciprocal association between parenting techniques or style and BPD symptoms in children. They reinforce one another. A study of 2,451 girls found that there is a link between two parenting factors and BPD: punishment and warmth.

The study tracked the girls and their parents over several years. Girls who showed the highest levels of BPD symptoms were also more likely to report that their parents were less warm and more inclined to use harsher punishments. The authors of the study concluded that these parenting practices trigger BPD symptoms, but BPD symptoms also seem to trigger particular parenting practices.[xxviii]

Let's see how this might unfold. Suppose a child has a mother who is stricter than the average parent and gets impatient easily when their son or daughter is upset or frustrated. The mother may punish their child for crying, perhaps telling them to "stop being silly" or to "stop crying, or I'll give you something to cry about!"

This kind of parenting teaches a child that expressing sadness is "bad," and if they share their sadness, they can expect to be punished. If a child happens to be born with a sensitive temperament, they will become sensitive or even nervous around their mother, making them more prone to emotional outbursts in the future, which will provoke their mother even further, and so the cycle continues. Eventually, the mother might decide that their child is "impossible" and needs to be treated even more harshly.

Exercise: What Kind Of Parents Did You Have?

You can appreciate the link between parenting style and BPD without becoming angry at your parents or blaming them for your problems. Think about how your parent(s) or other main caregiver acted when you were upset or anxious. Did they offer reassurance and validate your feelings, or did they make you feel abnormal or "wrong" for being unhappy?

THE BIOLOGY OF BPD

Scientists have discovered that the brains of people with BPD appear to work a little differently to the norm. So far, researchers know that serotonin and differences in the limbic system might explain some common BPD behaviors.

SEROTONIN

Serotonin, a type of chemical produced naturally in the brain, plays a key role in self-regulation. In simple terms, when our serotonin levels are in balance, we find it easier to regulate our feelings and stop ourselves from acting on destructive impulses.

Research with depressed and suicidal people shows a link between serotonin levels and depressive symptoms. As a general rule, if your brain produces lower than average amounts of serotonin, you are at elevated risk of depression. Rats with lower than average brain serotonin find it hard to suppress behaviors that they know will lead to punishment, such as electric shock.

In humans, people with a history of violent crimes or actions also have abnormally low serotonin levels. It isn't possible to measure serotonin levels directly, but it's possible to measure a byproduct called CSF 5-HIAA, which the body makes when it breaks down serotonin.[xxix]

People with BPD might be low in serotonin. This explains why they find it hard to learn from their mistakes, why they are prone to anger, and why they are vulnerable to depression. Their anger isn't always directed at other people. Often, people with BPD feel angrier with themselves than anyone else. Other research suggests that if you have BPD, the cells in your brain do not react normally to serotonin; they are less sensitive to serotonin than normal.

These differences may be caused by genetics, specifically, by the genes that control how much serotonin is produced by the brain and how quickly it is broken down. But experience also plays a role. Traumatic experiences can influence how well serotonin systems work (or rather, do not work).

BPD AND THE LIMBIC SYSTEM

People with BPD tend to have a negative bias towards the world—that is, they assume the worst. For instance, compared to people without BPD, they tend to see neutral faces as more threatening and to be more suspicious of other peoples' motives.[xxx] Their threat detection system is on high alert.

This might be because, in BPD, the limbic system does not work as it should. The limbic system is made up of several parts of the brain. These parts include the hippocampus, which is important for memory formation, and the amygdala, which helps us respond to frightening situations.

When the amygdala is stimulated in animals, they behave aggressively. When it is removed, wild animals become tame and show no fear. People with BPD have more sensitive amygdalae, which could explain why they are quicker to label something as a threat.

NATURE AND NURTURE: THE BIOSOCIAL MODEL OF BPD

The biosocial model of BPD suggests that there are two things that cause BPD that work together: emotional vulnerability, which is inborn and shaped by genetics, and an invalidating environment. This model was put forward by Dr. Marsha Linehan, who is considered one of the world's foremost experts on BPD.[xxxi]

EMOTIONAL VULNERABILITY

Some babies are born with a calm temperament, whereas others are fussier or seem slower to settle. The biosocial model suggests that people with the following traits are more emotionally vulnerable:

Sensitivity: Sensitive people are quick to react to their environment. They also have unusually intense emotions.

Trouble regulating intense emotions: Not only do sensitive people experience strong emotions, but they have trouble handling them.

Slow return to baseline: Think of the last time you had a strong emotional response to someone or something. However intense your emotion, it eventually faded away. This is called "returning to baseline." People with BPD take longer than average to return to a baseline state. They spend more time feeling distressed.

Later, Linehan recognized that impulsive tendencies are also an important part of the puzzle. Poor impulse control may explain why people with BPD often engage in risky behaviors and harm themselves.

INVALIDATING ENVIRONMENTS

Children raised in an invalidating environment are taught that their thoughts and feelings are illogical, undesirable, or "silly." For example, their parents may ignore the child's worries by telling them to forget about their troubles or react to their child's joy by telling them to calm down instead of joining in their happiness.

Being raised in an invalidating environment makes a child question themselves and their own judgment. If they are repeatedly told that their emotions are wrong, they learn that talking about how they feel isn't a good idea. If they aren't shown how to tolerate, identify, and communicate their emotions, they might develop unhealthy coping strategies that continue into their teen and adult years.

WHAT DOES INVALIDATION LOOK LIKE?

Invalidation can be subtle. A parent does not have to scream or hit a child to invalidate them. For example, eye-rolling and passive-aggressive remarks can still cause a lot of hurt for a sensitive child. Although all abusive relationships are invalidating, not all invalidating environments are abusive. An invalidating parent generally cannot or will not tolerate open displays of emotion in other people.

It's possible to mix praise with invalidation. For example, suppose a young child is nervous about going to a birthday party at a friend's house. They manage to attend the party and have a good time. When the child's mother picks them up, she says, "Well done. Bet you feel ridiculous for being worried now, right?" This type of praise appears supportive but actually makes the child feel bad or inferior for being anxious.

If you are a parent, rest assured that a few invalidating comments will not give your child BPD or another mental illness. No parent is perfect. Everyone makes a snappy or unsupportive remark occasionally. Only when a child is consistently undermined or made to feel inferior simply for having feelings can their home environment be called invalidating.

Sometimes, an unfortunate mismatch between parent and child can make the latter feel invalidated. A child who is born with an unusual sensitivity to emotions, and who tends to feel everything very keenly, can be a challenge for any parent. If the parent, despite trying their best, can't give the child enough validation, their son or daughter experiences their family environment as invalidating. Their parent might feel as though their child is unusually reactive and needs to be taught to behave "normally."[xxxii]

ATTACHMENT STYLE AND BPD

Most people with BPD crave relationships but worry about rejection and abandonment. If you have BPD, relationships probably cause you a lot of pain. The thought of someone leaving you might be too much to bear, and you even might have decided to avoid relationships entirely. Some psychologists believe that attachment theory can explain this reaction.

According to attachment theory, almost every human being is born with the desire to form positive, warm, affectionate bonds with our caregivers. These are called attachments. A secure attachment makes a baby feel loved and safe. The attachment between the baby and their caregiver forms a template for the baby's later relationships. If their caregiver makes them feel reassured and treats them kindly, they will grow up feeling as though they are a decent and worthwhile human being. If not, they may grow up with an unhealthy idea of what relationships with other people should be like and will form unhealthy attachments with other people as adults.

People with BPD often find it hard to tolerate being alone. According to some psychologists, this might be explained by the type of attachment they formed with their primary caregiver. Babies who are securely attached to their caregiver grow up with a sense of safety. Even when no one else is around, they still feel as though they are basically "OK" and that the world is a safe place.

Unfortunately, children who do not have this kind of secure attachment do not feel this way. For them, to be alone is to be without any care, and the idea of depending on themselves is overwhelming. When they grow up and form attachments to others, they cannot feel safe.

THE FOUR ATTACHMENT STYLES AND BPD

There are four main attachment styles: secure, ambivalent, avoidant, and disordered.[xxxiii] We'll look at each in turn.

People with a **secure attachment style** were raised by caregivers who were reliable, attentive, and loving. They grow up with a positive self-image. They believe that they are worthy of love, and assume that if they treat other people well, they will get the same in return.

A child with a secure attachment style feels distressed if their caregiver leaves them alone, and feels happy and reassured when they come back. They see their caregiver as a "safe base," and when they are around, they feel happy exploring a new environment or meeting new people.

Children with an **ambivalent attachment style** are uneasy around strangers when left alone by their parents, but do not seem relieved when their parent returns. Sometimes they might even reject their parent's attempts to comfort them. These children grow up to be adults who are slow to develop close ties with others, who often worry that their feelings for other people aren't returned, and who become very upset when a relationship ends.

People with an **avoidant attachment style** tend to be wary of other people, assuming they will make unreasonable demands or become clingy. They are reluctant to open up about their thoughts and feelings and hesitate to form meaningful relationships. Raised by parents who couldn't or wouldn't meet their emotional needs, they never learned how to be emotionally intimate with someone without becoming overwhelmed. They are aloof and reluctant to ask for help in times of need. They value their independence and are slow to trust other people.

Finally, those with a **disorganized attachment style** are erratic when it comes to interacting with others. Sometimes they want to avoid other people, but at times they can also be clingy and dependent. A disorganized attachment style might be the result of inconsistent parenting. If a parent is warm and reassuring one moment, then cold and frightening the next, the child will become confused and unsure how to act in relationships.

Only 6-8% of people with BPD have a secure attachment style,[xxxiv] compared with 58% of the general population,[xxxv] which supports the theory that a lot of BPD symptoms are linked with insecure attachment. A review of 13 studies on this subject found that people with BPD are typically worried about being rejected by others, while also longing for emotional intimacy.[xxxvi]

Exercise: Do You Have A Secure Adult Attachment Style?

A secure attachment style doesn't guarantee happy relationships, but it helps. Here are the key signs of a securely attached adult: They show empathy, they are not abusive, they know how and when to compromise, they have healthy boundaries, they are not prone to jealousy, and they are not afraid to commit to people they love.

If this describes you, congratulations—you probably have a secure attachment style. If not, don't worry. Attachment styles are not set in stone. If you are willing to work on your relationship and communication skills, you can change.

It's possible to change your attachment style. With the right treatment, you can learn how to form healthier relationships and learn to balance closeness with independence.

THE LINK BETWEEN CHILD ABUSE AND BPD

Childhood abuse does not always cause BPD, and not everyone with BPD is a victim of childhood abuse. However, there is a lot of evidence that many people—at least half—of people with BPD were abused as children. [xxxvii] Abuse can be physical, emotional, or sexual. It can also take the form of neglect.

What might explain the link between abuse and BPD? Some psychologists have narrowed down the question further and looked at whether experiencing abuse has an effect on an individual's ability to regulate their emotions. This is important because people who have trouble regulating their emotions tend to act impulsively, which is a core problem in BPD. Impulsivity is linked to poor coping strategies, self-harm, suicide attempts, poor self-image, and unsteady relationships. [xxxviii]

A study with 178 women—61 with BPD, 60 healthy controls, and 57 with other psychiatric conditions—found that the participants who experienced the most severe abuse as children had the most problems regulating their emotions and were more prone to impulsive behaviors. This was true whether they had BPD, another mental health problem, or no mental health conditions at all.

For women with BPD, there was a much stronger link between abuse and impulsivity. The more abuse they had suffered, the more impulsive they were. However, after the researchers had controlled for emotional regulation difficulties, this effect disappeared. In other words, people with BPD are more likely to have been abused as children, but this abuse doesn't in itself make them impulsive; it causes emotional dysregulation, which in turn leads to impulsivity.

Another piece of research backs up this finding. A survey of 243 students found a positive correlation between frequency of emotional abuse in childhood and BPD symptom severity. [xxxix]

CHILDHOOD BULLYING AND **BPD**

Abuse by adults predicts BPD symptoms later in life, but experiencing peer abuse can also raise your risk. One study with 6,050 children found that those who are chronically bullied are more likely to develop BPD symptoms than those who enjoy positive relationships with their classmates.[xl]

Another piece of research, this time with 414 adults, found that being bullied at school correlates positively with BPD symptoms. Being bullied also correlates with unhealthy behaviors, including binge eating, road rage, excessive spending, and substance misuse.[xli]

The take-home message: BPD doesn't have a single cause

In summary, BPD isn't a mental illness that suddenly develops in late adolescence or young adulthood. It is a set of behaviors and thought processes that begin in childhood; it's a product of environmental, genetic, and social factors. It's impossible to identify the exact cause in every case.

Exercise: What Do You Think Caused Your Symptoms?

Having read through this chapter, do you have a better idea of what might have caused or triggered your BPD?

Understanding the causes of BPD is empowering. If you have been diagnosed, learning how your childhood could have affected your mental health can bring a sense of relief. On the other hand, you don't need to work out precisely what caused your symptoms. It's more important that you remain focused on the present and concentrate on getting help.

SUMMARY

- BPD is a complex disorder with several potential causes.
- Researchers believe that biological and social factors contribute to BPD.
- The biosocial model of BPD suggests that some children are born with an unusually sensitive temperament and, if they grow up in an invalidating environment, they may develop BPD.
- You may not know exactly what caused your BPD. This isn't a problem—what's more important is that you get the help you need right now to live a better life.

CHAPTER 4:

PSYCHOTHERAPY FOR BPD

n this chapter, we're going to look at the types of talking therapy you might be offered if you have BPD. Because everyone is different, there is no single treatment that works perfectly for everyone. You might have to try more than one approach before you find something that helps you feel better.

The five most common types of therapy for BPD, known in the world of psychiatry as "the big 5," are:[xlii]

- Dialectical Behavior Therapy (DBT)
- Mentalization-Based Therapy (MBT)
- Transference-Focused Psychotherapy (TFP)
- Schema-Focused Psychotherapy (SFT)
- Good Psychiatric Management (GPM)

Psychotherapy involves talking about problems, identifying and teaching new coping mechanisms, and helping someone understand how their thoughts, emotions, and behaviors influence one another.

BPD treatment takes a long time, generally between one and three years. This is because the thought patterns and behaviors in someone with BPD are deeply entrenched. Breaking old habits, learning to regulate one's emotions, and practicing new coping skills requires persistence.

Some of these therapies are given on a one-to-one basis, others are delivered in group sessions, and some use a mixture of both. While psychotherapy for other mental health conditions, such as depression and anxiety, normally require one session per week, it's not uncommon for someone with BPD to have two or three sessions per week.

Dialectical Behavior Therapy (DBT)

This is the best-known therapy for BPD and has been used since the 1980s. DBT is based on the assumption that people with BPD tend to have more intense emotional reactions to both minor and major life events. DBT is a practical form of therapy that teaches patients how to recognize and cope with their emotions.

It also challenges the type of thinking that keeps BPD symptoms going. For example, people with BPD often see the world in a very black and white way. To them, people, things, and events are either "good" or "bad," with nothing in between. DBT equips people with the ability to slow down and evaluate things in a more realistic way.

DBT is also a supportive form of therapy. During DBT sessions, patients are encouraged to think about the positive traits and skills they already have. Therapists don't criticize their patients; they hold them accountable for their own development, but they stay warm and supportive.

There are two parts of DBT: individual sessions and group therapy sessions. Both take place once per week.

During **individual sessions,** therapists help clients work on recent problems, such as self-injury and ongoing trouble in relationships. Together, they come up with problem-solving strategies the client can use to improve their quality of life. Clients can also contact their therapist between sessions if they need extra support. These sessions usually last around an hour.

During **group therapy sessions,** which are two to three hours long, a trained DBT therapist leads discussion sessions focusing on skills to improve emotional regulation and relationships.

There are four "modules" that make up DBT. These skills are taught in group sessions. They are:[xliii]

1. **Mindfulness**

    This is the core skill that underpins the other modules. To be mindful is to notice and describe whatever is going on in the present moment without thinking about the past, worrying about the future, or getting caught up in negative thoughts and ideas.

2. **Interpersonal Effectiveness**

    This module includes skills that help build good relationships, including assertiveness training and conflict resolution. If you have BPD, you probably have unstable relationships. Learning these skills will help you make and keep friendships, get along better with colleagues, and improve your romantic relationships.

    Interpersonal effectiveness skills help you get what you want from relationships while respecting the rights and wishes of other people. They help you develop balanced, enjoyable relationships built on mutual respect.

3. **Distress Tolerance**

    Because people with BPD have more intense emotions than the average person, they find it difficult to tolerate their own distress. Distress tolerance skills teach you how to accept reality, how to soothe yourself, how to distract yourself from whatever is causing you distress, how to improve things in the present moment, and how to think rationally about the pros and cons of a situation.

Accepting a situation—known as "radical acceptance" in DBT—does not mean approving of it. You can accept something just as it is, without trying to change it.

4. Emotion Regulation

Mood swings are a common problem for people with BPD. Emotion regulation skills are useful for anyone who struggles to acknowledge, identify, and manage their feelings. If you find it hard to keep your emotions under control, these skills will teach you how to feel more balanced.

This module teaches participants how to label their feelings, how to help themselves feel more positive, how to apply distress tolerance techniques when they feel overwhelmed, how to approach emotions in a mindful way, and how to avoid giving into emotion-driven, rather than rational, thinking.

THE STAGES OF DBT

The pre-treatment stage: The client agrees to commit to therapy, normally for at least one year. DBT isn't a quick fix, and it isn't always a pleasant process. To be successful, a client needs to be willing to examine their own behavior, to be challenged by other people, and to work in collaboration with their therapist.

Stage 1: The therapist's first priority is to address suicidal behaviors and self-injury. This stage also focuses on "therapy-interfering" behaviors, including being late to sessions, refusing to do homework, and being passive-aggressive towards the therapist or other people in group therapy sessions.

This stage also involves tackling behaviors that lower a client's quality of life. For example, if a client drinks a lot of alcohol or abuses prescription drugs, this issue needs to be addressed.

Stage 2: If a client has a history of trauma, it is addressed at this point in therapy.

Stage 3: At Stage 3, the therapist works with the client to raise the client's self-esteem and work towards their personal treatment goals. For example, a client might set for themself the goal of getting a job or going back to college.

These stages are always applied in this sequence. They provide the therapist with a reliable framework that helps them focus on their client's problems in a logical order. This is useful when working with BPD clients, who often have several problems that need to be addressed.

MENTALIZATION-BASED THERAPY (MBT)

Mentalizing means understanding how your feelings, beliefs, desires, and thoughts work together to influence your behaviors and relationships. To mentalize also means to imagine or work out—to the best of your ability, with the information you have available—what other people might be thinking or feeling. Mentalization skills can improve your relationships, and MBT is particularly useful for people who find it hard to trust others. It usually lasts between 12 and 18 months and is delivered in individual or weekly sessions.

MBT is based on the assumption that people with BPD missed a crucial developmental milestone as young children: being able to think about and judge one's own mental state and feelings. This is more likely if their parents didn't emotionally engage with them or teach them how to recognize and cope with emotions.

If a parent is inconsistent—for example, appearing tolerant and kind one day, then irrational and brusque the next for no apparent reason—their child will be confused because there are no obvious links among the parent's communication style, emotions, and behaviors. The child misses out on opportunities to learn how people think and behave. This can leave them feeling confused about their own emotions and thoughts, and leave them prone to relationship difficulties as they get older.

Some people with BPD had parents who didn't mirror them. In developmental psychology, to "mirror" a child is to reflect their mental state. For example, a father who mirrors his daughter's anxious state might frown slightly and purse his lips in concern while saying, "Oh dear, are you worried? I know you must be scared." Mirroring comes naturally to most parents, and it serves a key purpose in their children's development. It teaches a child how to express and discuss their feelings. In other words, it helps them develop the ability to mentalize.

MBT helps clients learn how to identify their emotions and keep them under control. Clients who can manage their feelings are less likely to act impulsively. When the client is more stable, they can then start to address the way they think about themselves and others. The therapist acts as a mirror. They validate the client's feelings, helping them practice putting their emotions into words.

MBT is not a highly structured therapy like DBT. How they choose to explore the idea of mentalization is up to them. One common technique is to simply ask the client to describe their current mental state, a task that is often hard for people with BPD to accomplish.

The therapist does not pretend to be an expert on their clients' experiences. They remain deliberately open to new perspectives and never judge their clients, even if their thoughts and behaviors are illogical.[xliv] They encourage their clients to talk openly about how they think the therapy process is going. The relationship between the client and their therapist needs to be based on mutual trust for the treatment to work. MBT therapists don't offer practical solutions to their clients' problems. Instead, they help their clients improve their self-awareness and relationship skills so they can find their own solutions.

This form of therapy can be challenging. If you decide to try it, you need to be prepared to think and talk about events and people that have triggered strong negative emotions for you. If you are having group therapy, you will need to speak openly about your experiences, which can be scary. However, it might come as a big relief to discover that others face similar problems.

TRANSFERENCE-FOCUSED PSYCHOTHERAPY (TFP)

Like DBT, TFP was developed with BPD in mind. It was devised by Otto Kernberg, a psychiatrist and psychoanalyst. Psychoanalysts practice a type of talking therapy called psychoanalysis, which is based on the assumption that everyone has a conscious and unconscious mind. They believe that conflicts between these two parts cause distress and mental illness.

According to this theory, a patient will be cured of their problems when they can understand the unconscious thoughts and feelings that cause their destructive, unhelpful behaviors. Because the contents of the unconscious mind are usually hidden, psychoanalysts believe that patients need help to bring them to the surface where they can be explored in a safe environment. Psychoanalytic techniques include dream analysis and free association, where patients are encouraged to talk about their childhood memories.

Psychoanalysts are interested in how a person's past, especially their childhood, shapes their personality and mental health as an adult. For example, if a young child loses a parent, this might leave them vulnerable to depression as an adult if they don't come to terms with their loss.

Kernberg noticed that psychoanalysis was not very effective for patients with personality disorders. In his opinion, the problem was that traditional psychoanalysis did not pay enough attention to the internal representations we form of ourselves and other people in our early years.

He believed that when we are infants, we form two mental images or representations of our primary caregiver, which is usually our mother. When a baby feels happy and contented in the company of their mother, they see their mother as "good." When they feel sad, anxious, or otherwise uncomfortable, they experience their mother as "bad."

Kernberg thought that healthy adults learn to combine these experiences so that "good mommy" and "bad mommy" simply become "mommy." People with BPD do not learn how to do this. [xlv] Like small children, they continue to see their caregiver and everyone else in black and white terms, which explains why their relationships are volatile.

What Happens During TFP?

During TFP sessions, the therapist pays close attention to how the client presents themself and interacts with the therapist. The self-destructive behaviors and thoughts that cause a client so many problems outside the therapy room will also show up during sessions with a therapist. Sessions are usually individual and are held twice per week. TFP lasts at least one year because forming a strong, enduring therapeutic relationship is a key part of the therapy.

In the world of psychotherapy, "transference" is the term used to describe what is happening when a client re-enacts old relationship dynamics with their therapist. For example, suppose a client grew up with a mother who often showed anger and disapproval. If the client is wary around the therapist and constantly worries that the therapist will get angry, the client may be transferring the patterns from that relationship into the therapy room.

When a therapist notices that their client might be engaging in transference, they can bring it to the client's attention. By sharing their observations, the therapist can start encouraging the client to re-examine how they approach relationships. To continue with the example above, the client and therapist could work together to help the client build self-esteem and become less dependent on other people for validation.

Just as a young child must learn how to combine "good mommy" and "bad mommy" representations, the client needs to combine their "good therapist" and "bad therapist" representations instead of seeing the therapist as either all good or all bad. TFP therapists encourage their clients to be open with their feelings. Anger and resentment in the therapy room are powerful tools for healing.

Therapists encourage their clients to seek training or employment, to develop new interests, or to volunteer their time for a good cause. If a client has another problem, such as an alcohol abuse disorder, they can receive other treatment alongside TFP.

SCHEMA-FOCUSED PSYCHOTHERAPY (SFT)

A schema is a set of ideas and expectations about a particular person, place, process, or object. For example, for most people, a restaurant schema would include ideas about tables, chairs, menus, food, chefs, and kitchens. Schemas are useful because they provide us with social scripts that help us decide how to behave in everyday life.

We don't just have schemas about the external world. We also have a set of ideas about who we are and how we relate to others. This is called a self-schema. Ideally, self-schemas are positive. If you have a positive self-schema, you acknowledge that although you have faults and have made mistakes, you are a worthwhile person who deserves to be happy.

Negative, unhelpful schemas can hold you back from developing good relationships and building a healthy sense of self.

1. **Emotional deprivation schema**
   Typical beliefs: "No one is capable of meeting my emotional needs. No one understands me."
   Result: You avoid relationships because they believe there is no one in the world who could understand and respect you. You might stay too long in an abusive or unfulfilling relationship because you believe you won't be able to find a better match.

2. **Enmeshment schema**

   Typical beliefs: "I can't possibly be content or meet my goals unless I have the complete support of my friends, family, and partner. I can't rely on myself for anything."

   Result: You have a terrible fear of criticism that keeps you from trying new things. You may become resentful towards your family or friends for not supporting your dreams.

3. **Defectiveness schema**

   Typical beliefs: "There is something fundamentally wrong with me. I am unlovable. If someone accepts me, it's only because they haven't figured out what I'm really like. I may as well abandon my partner first before they abandon me."

   Result: You stop pursuing relationships with others. If you believe you are unlovable and somehow defective, you won't be able to believe that someone else will want to be with you.

4. **Social isolation schema**

   Typical beliefs: "No one accepts me. I am all alone in the world."

   Result: You isolate yourself. You stop trying to make friends and resist opening up to others, assuming that they will reject you. A social isolation schema is a self-fulfilling prophecy.

5. **Failure schema**

   Typical beliefs: "Everything I do goes wrong. I procrastinate all the time, and I never get anything done. I have no belief in myself; I'll never be a success."

Result: You don't trust your own judgment, so you are reluctant to take risks, learn, and grow. You feel dejected and depressed because you do not live up to your high standards (which may be unrealistic).

6. **Emotional deprivation schema**
   Typical beliefs: "No one ever supports me when I feel bad. There is a chronic emptiness in my life. I can't share how I feel with anyone. I have never been anyone's first choice or felt special."

   Result: You feel distant from others, even when spending time with them. You feel lonely within your relationships. It seems as though no one understands you.

Exercise: Do These Schemas Sound Familiar?

Many people with BPD use the schemas in this list. What about you? Do you tend to fall into these thought patterns?
During sessions, a therapist works with the client to uncover unhelpful schemas the client holds about themself and the world. The therapist will ask the client how they perceive and handle situations. The client's answers give the therapist insight into their thought processes. By challenging these patterns, the client can approach life and its challenges in a more constructive way. BPD clients may use many unhelpful schemas, and months of therapy might be required to challenge them.

GOOD PSYCHIATRIC MANAGEMENT (GPM)

Some psychiatrists have suggested that not everyone with BPD needs specialized therapies such as DBT. They argue that weekly support sessions with a mental health professional are enough for many cases. These sessions, which include case management and supportive psychotherapy, are referred to as good psychiatric management, or GPM.

Case management is a way of helping clients deal with life problems. For example, for a client struggling to cope with holding down a job, case management can be used to help them find ways of handling stress at work.

Supportive psychotherapy is a broad term, but usually it is used to describe any form of talking therapy that helps a client understand themself and adopt better coping mechanisms in the face of stress.

Here are the basic principles: [xlvi]

1. **The mental health professional doing GPM should gently challenge a client's problematic behaviors.**

   For example, if they are treating a BPD patient who claims to want recovery yet doesn't do anything to change their situation, they should ask them to come up with actionable goals.

2. **The professional should show genuine interest in the patient's life and reassure them that their experiences are valid.**

   People with BPD often grew up with parents who invalidated their emotions, so knowing that their doctors and therapists are taking them seriously is important.

3. **The professional should encourage the patient to "get a life."**

   This means obtaining a job or getting an education before focusing on relationships. GPM is a practical approach.

It assumes that you can work on coping and relationship skills while overhauling other areas of your life.

Many people with BPD are preoccupied with relationships, and their relationships are often dysfunctional, dramatic, and time-consuming. This leaves little room in their lives for work. A regular job or college course can offer more structure and validation than a relationship.

4. **The professional should form a genuine relationship with their patient.**

   They should not look down on, or lecture, the patient. If it's appropriate, they can share their personal experiences and feelings. For instance, if their patient tells them a sad story, it would be reasonable for the professional to say something like, "That sounds very upsetting; it would have made me sad too."

5. **The professional should expect change.**

   GPM should strike a balance between validating patients and pushing them to improve. If the patient shows no signs of change, the professional must evaluate whether GPM is the right treatment.

6. **The professional should encourage the patient to be accountable for their progress, symptom management, and seeking extra help when they need it.**

   For example, if the patient feels their condition is declining, they should adhere to any crisis plan they have drawn up in advance with their doctor.

   Psychoeducation is another key part of GPM. Patients learn about BPD, including its causes, symptoms, and the ways it progresses. They may be given books or leaflets to read between sessions. They are encouraged to think of themselves as people who have a medical condition that can be properly managed.

Some mental health professionals choose to involve a patient's family in their sessions (with the patient's consent) if doing so would be useful. For example, if a patient lives with someone who does not understand what BPD is or how it is treated, an education session could help everyone reach a shared understanding.

Although it is unrealistic to expect that every single person with BPD or another mental illness will eventually have a full-time job and a stable relationship, the majority of patients can and do recover. Even if a particular individual cannot live a "normal" life, they are still encouraged to strive for self-acceptance and contentment.

Research shows that many mental health professionals are wary of BPD patients, but more than 1 in 5 people they see have the condition. Fortunately, professionals who have been trained in the basics of GPM—which only takes one day for people who already have some mental health training—feel more confident treating BPD and hold fewer negative views about the illness.

WHICH THERAPY IS BEST?

Research comparing the success rates of these therapies suggests that they all have similar success rates. Around half (40-60%) of BPD patients significantly improve after treatment, meaning their symptoms become a lot more manageable, and they stop meeting the criteria for BPD.[xlvii]

When choosing a treatment, you'll need to take into account what's available in your area, your budget (some programs and therapists will be more expensive than others), your insurance coverage, and your preferences. For example, you might prefer the idea of one-on-one sessions over group therapy. Your doctor, psychiatrist, or social worker is the best person to ask for recommendations.

SUMMARY

- Psychotherapy is the most popular treatment for BPD.
- The five most commonly used approaches are Dialectical Behavior Therapy (DBT), Mentalization-Based Therapy (MBT), Transference-Focused Psychotherapy (TFP), Schema-Focused Psychotherapy (SFT), and Good Psychiatric Management (GPM).
- All of these therapies have shown positive results in research studies.

CHAPTER 5:

MEDICATION & BPD

No drug can cure BPD, and psychotherapy is the gold standard treatment. But in many cases, psychiatrists will prescribe medication to their BPD patients. In this chapter, you'll learn about the different types of medication you might be offered, how they work, and why most doctors think drugs should be used along with—not instead of—therapy.

Is Medication Widely Used?

Between 90% and 99% of people with BPD are prescribed medication.[xlviii] Its efficacy is a matter of debate in the world of psychiatry. Of the studies that have been done in this area, most have limitations such as small sample sizes and high dropout rates.[xlix] They also tend to be short-term. In most studies, participants are followed for only a few weeks or months. This means that we don't have much information about the long-term effects of medication on BPD.

Medication options include mood stabilizers, antipsychotic medications, antidepressants, and anxiolytics. They don't start to work immediately. Depending on the drug, you may need to wait several weeks before seeing the benefits.

MOOD STABILIZERS

As the name implies, these drugs reduce mood swings and dampen extreme emotions. The most popular medications in this category include lamotrigine, valproate, lithium, carbamazepine, and topiramate. They work by regulating abnormal brain activity.

They can also reduce impulsive behavior, which in turn can reduce the risk of self-harm. Some of these drugs are also anticonvulsants that are used to treat epilepsy. There is some promising evidence that these drugs work well, but there haven't been many high-quality studies on their long-term effects.[1]

ANTIPSYCHOTIC MEDICATION

Paranoia in BPD is usually triggered by a stressful situation. Once the stress passes, so does the paranoia. There are lots of things you can do to help yourself if this is an issue for you, including breathing exercises, distracting yourself, meditation, or simply waiting for the feelings to subside.

But some people find that paranoia becomes an ongoing problem and choose to take medication to manage their symptoms. Antipsychotic drugs such as risperidone, haloperidol, clozapine, and olanzapine reduce paranoia, hostility, impulsive behaviors, and anxiety.[li]

These drugs work by blocking dopamine in the brain. Most mental health professionals believe that psychosis is caused by excessive dopamine levels, so by blocking it, antipsychotic drugs can reduce psychotic symptoms. They also regulate the amount of serotonin and other brain chemicals.

ANTIDEPRESSANTS AND **BPD**

Lots of people with BPD report feeling sad, low, empty, and anxious. Antidepressants, including bupropion, sertraline, fluoxetine, and phenelzine, can reduce these symptoms.

There are several types of antidepressants:

Selective serotonin reuptake inhibitors (SSRIs): These drugs make your brain more receptive to its own serotonin, which can improve your mood.

Tricyclic antidepressants (TCAs): These are an older class of antidepressants that aren't prescribed as often as SSRIs. They are most often prescribed for people with severe depression who have not responded to SSRIs and work by increasing levels of serotonin and norepinephrine in the brain. They include amitriptyline, clomipramine, lofepramine, and imipramine.

Monoamine oxidase inhibitors (MAOIs): Another older class of drug, MAOIs have been around since the 1950s. Monoamine oxidase is an enzyme that breaks down dopamine, norepinephrine, and serotonin. These neurotransmitters all play a role in regulating mood. By changing the levels of these chemicals in the brain, MAOIs reduce anxiety and have a positive effect on overall mood.

They are as effective as other types of antidepressants, but they are prescribed less often. This is because they don't mix well with some types of food and medication. They can be taken as pills or via a skin patch that slowly releases the drug into the bloodstream. Isocarboxazid, tranylcypromine, and phenelzine are the most widely used.

Atypical antidepressants: There are a few other antidepressants that don't fit into the above categories. They work by changing one or more of the neurotransmitters that affect mood, including serotonin, dopamine, and norepinephrine. Trazodone, esketamine, mirtazapine, and nefazodone are four such drugs.

Antidepressants can blunt the symptoms of depression, but they can't take away any underlying causes; you will still need to undergo therapy. For example, you might feel depressed because living with BPD is very challenging and might have cost you a good job opportunity or caused your relationship to break down. You need to confront the events that triggered your depression.

ANXIOLYTICS

More commonly known as anti-anxiety medication, these drugs are prescribed to some people with BPD who have problems with anxiety. They include buspirone, lorazepam, and diazepam. Some anxiolytics change the way your brain responds to dopamine and serotonin. Others make your brain more sensitive to a chemical called GABA, a neurotransmitter that has a calming effect on brain activity.

Unfortunately, there isn't much evidence to suggest that they work particularly well. In fact, some research shows that they can make BPD symptoms worse.[lii] Some of these drugs belong to a class of medication known as benzodiazepines, or "benzos." They can be habit-forming, so they are not usually recommended for anyone with a substance abuse disorder.

SIDE EFFECTS

Medication can cause many unpleasant side effects, including high blood pressure, confusion, muscle spasms, insomnia, fatigue, sexual dysfunction, anxiety, skin rash, weight gain, dizziness, nausea, nightmares, and dry mouth. Side effects can be mild, moderate, or severe. If your side effects are particularly bad, your doctor will change your medication. Sometimes side effects go away within a few weeks.

Very occasionally, antidepressants can cause suicidal thoughts and behaviors. The risk is higher for young people, and the side effects usually show up within the first three months of treatment.[liii] Get help immediately if you are having suicidal thoughts.

It's common for people with BPD to have one or more other mental health problems. Some people take multiple medications (for example, an antidepressant and a mood stabilizer), but psychiatrists prefer their patients to take the least possible number of drugs.

Never stop taking your medication without consulting your doctor. Sudden withdrawal can be unpleasant or even dangerous. You might need to taper your medication over a few days or weeks, depending on your dose and how long you've been taking it. If you've stopped taking your medication, never restart it again without getting medical advice first.

Exercise: Talking To Your Doctor About Medication

If you are offered medication, make sure you understand the pros and cons when deciding whether it's right for you. Here are some questions you might want to ask your doctor:

- *Why do you recommend this particular medication?*
- *What are the common side effects?*
- *[If you are female] If I want to get pregnant, will this medication have any effect on my baby?*
- *How long will I have to take this medication?*
- *How often will I need to see you for a medication review?*

- *Will I need any blood tests to check the levels of medication in my blood?*
- *Do I need to avoid any particular foods with this medication? Can I drink alcohol?*

What Happens if Therapy and Medication Don't Work?

For most people with BPD, therapy and medication can keep their symptoms under control. But these treatments aren't always enough.

Hospitalization

You might have to go to the hospital if you are in danger of hurting yourself or other people, or if you need treatment that can only be given in a hospital setting. Being hospitalized can be scary, but fear is usually worse than reality.

If you choose to go to the hospital on your doctor's advice, this is called voluntary admission. If your doctor believes that you need a high level of care that can't be provided outside of a hospital setting, but you don't agree, you can be admitted on an involuntary basis. This is sometimes called "commitment" or "being committed to the hospital."

When you go to the hospital, your treatment team will aim to stabilize your condition and keep you safe. For example, if you have been admitted to the hospital because you are planning to commit suicide, you will be released when the doctors decide your life is no longer in danger. While you're in the hospital, you might attend regular group therapy sessions, individual therapy sessions, or both. You might be prescribed new or additional medication. You will usually be allowed visitors, although visiting hours are typically limited.

After you've been discharged from inpatient care, you may be referred to a day hospital program. These programs require you to come into the hospital for several hours each day, but you are allowed to go home in the evening. A partial program can bridge the gap between inpatient treatment and a normal routine.

Doctors try to avoid sending people to the hospital, and the staff will try to release you as soon as possible. There is no evidence that long stays in the hospital are helpful. In general, it's best for people with mental health problems to live at home and stick to a normal routine if they can. Even in a well-run ward with caring staff, a hospital is a stressful place, and stress often makes BPD symptoms worse.

Summary

- There are no drugs licensed specifically to treat BPD.
- Doctors sometimes prescribe medication to treat some of the symptoms of BPD, such as mood swings.
- Antidepressants, antianxiety medication, and antipsychotic drugs are used to treat the symptoms of BPD. Some are well-established, while others are relatively new.
- Doctors try to prescribe the minimum necessary number of drugs.
- Never stop taking your medication or adjust the dose without checking in with your doctor.
- Only therapy, not medication, can change deep-seated thought patterns and beliefs that underpin serious BPD symptoms.
- If medication and therapy aren't keeping your symptoms under control, you may need to be stabilized in the hospital.

CHAPTER 6:

COMPLEMENTARY & ALTERNATIVE TREATMENTS FOR BPD

Prescription medication and talking therapies are evidence based treatments. This means they have been tested in rigorous scientific trials that have been designed and reviewed by medical experts. But this doesn't mean they work for everyone, and neither does it mean that everyone wants to try them. For example, some people find the side effects of medication so unpleasant that they would rather live with their symptoms.

Complementary and alternative treatments seem to help reduce symptoms of mental health problems for some patients. "Complementary" treatments are used alongside conventional medicine. "Alternative" treatments are used instead of mainstream treatments. Most people use the terms interchangeably, however.

Some use the term "CAMs," which stands for Complementary and Alternative Medicines, to refer to remedies that come in the form of supplements, pills, foods, and other consumables.

There are no specific CAMs for BPD. Just like conventional medicine, they are used for specific symptoms, such as anxiety and depression.

Let's look at some of the most popular alternative and complementary treatments, how they are used, and their potential side effects.

YOGA

Yoga is a set of practices and philosophies that originated in ancient India. It's now popular in western countries, where it's used as a form of exercise rather than a form of spirituality. You don't need to hold any particular belief systems to practice yoga. Most classes and online videos focus on poses, stretches, and general wellbeing.

Yoga helps you appreciate your body. It also strengthens your mind-body connection, keeping you grounded in the present rather than the past or future. It's beneficial for people who dissociate. If you have experienced trauma or abuse, yoga can give you back a sense of bodily control and autonomy.

Yoga also teaches you to be more mindful. Therapies like Dialectical Behavior Therapy (DBT), which have been proven to help reduce BPD symptoms, place a lot of emphasis on mindfulness as a skill. Mindfulness is a great stress reliever. Studies with patients staying on psychiatric wards show that taking part in yoga classes can improve your mood.[liv]

As long as you use common sense, yoga is a safe exercise that is great for your body and mind. Going to a yoga class also could help you make new friends; when you meet new people at a class, you know you already have something in common. It's a great way to start building new, healthy relationships.

Exercise: A Simple Yoga Pose

Yoga doesn't have to be complicated. Try this exercise, known as Bridge Pose:

Lie on your back. If your shoulders are uncomfortable, rest them on a cushion or folded blanket. Bend your knees. Keep your feet flat on the floor. Exhale and gently clench your buttocks while pushing your pelvis upward so that your body forms the shape of a bridge. Straighten your arms and clasp your hands together on the floor underneath your pelvis. Keep your feet and thighs parallel. Hold the pose for 30-60 seconds. Exhale and gently lower yourself to the floor. Search online for free yoga videos for lots more poses you can do at home or at work.

MASSAGE

Like yoga, massage is physically and emotionally nourishing. It can help relieve anxiety, insomnia, and pain.[lv] The kind of nurturing touch you get during a massage can be comforting—it lets you connect with another person in a safe environment.

Be careful when choosing your massage therapist. It's best to ask your doctor or therapist for recommendations. If you want to find one by yourself, make sure they hold a valid license to practice in your country or state. Ask them about their training and experience. A good therapist won't mind answering your questions.

Some forms of massage require you to remove some of your clothing. For example, if you want an aromatherapy massage using oils or a hot stone massage that involves direct skin contact, you'll have to remove your shirt. If you have a history of abuse or trauma, these types of massages might not be right for you. Ask the massage therapist in advance whether you'll need to undress. Some types of massage, such as Shiatsu and Thai massage, don't require you to remove any of your clothing.

Exercise: Give Yourself A Head Massage

Don't have the time or money to get a professional massage? No problem. With a bit of practice, you can become your own massage therapist. Using your fingers and thumbs, massage both sides of your head directly above your ears and work your way to the top. Massage the front of your head, then the back. Use a firm, rhythmic motion. Use the heels of your hands to apply pressure to your temples, using broad circular movements. Extend the massage to the back of your neck and shoulders for further stress relief.

AROMATHERAPY

Aromatherapy, also known as essential oil therapy, uses natural plant extracts to relieve symptoms. There is some evidence that it can help reduce anxiety, even among people with serious illness.[lvi] Lavender is a popular aromatherapy plant. The oil is cheap, smells good, and is easy to buy from pharmacies and health food stores.

Here's how you can use oils:

- Place a few drops of undiluted oil on a cotton wool ball and place it on your bedside table overnight.
- Unscrew the lid of a bottle of undiluted oil and take a few deep breaths.
- Dilute the oil in a carrier oil (such as almond or coconut oil) and rub it into your skin. Add 15 drops of neat oil to an ounce of carrier oil. You can then apply it to your face and body, but keep it away from your eyes, mouth, and any patches of irritated skin.
- Invest in a diffuser that heats essential oils and water and diffuses the mixture as a mist.

Some people are allergic to plant extracts. Remember, natural doesn't necessarily mean safe. If you have any side effects, such as a rash or difficulty breathing, stop using the oil and see your doctor. Because lavender and other oils can have a sedative effect, get medical advice before using it if you take any medication that makes you feel sleepy.

OMEGA-3 FATTY ACIDS

Omega-3 fatty acids are a type of unsaturated fats. They are sometimes called "essential fatty acids" because your body can't make them, so it's essential that you include them in your diet. Natural sources of omega-3 fatty acids include herring, mackerel, cod liver oil, chia seeds, and flax seeds. According to the World Health Organization (WHO), we should aim to eat two or more portions of oily fish every week.

Some research suggests omega-3 can help people with other mental health conditions. Omega-3 consumption can improve symptoms of depression and anxiety, help prevent psychosis, and stabilize mood in people with bipolar disorder.[lvii] It might also help people with BPD who have similar symptoms.

If you don't eat many foods that are high in omega-3, consider taking a supplement. Look for a supplement that contains both docosahexaenoic acid (DHA) and eicosapentaenoic acid (EPA), the two most useful types of omega-3 fats. A minimum of 250mg and a maximum of 500mg per day is a reasonable dose.

Exercise: An Omega-3 Shopping List

If you don't get many Omega-3 fatty acids in your diet, how can you squeeze them in? This week, set yourself a goal of trying at least one of the sources listed above.

ST. JOHN'S WORT

St. John's Wort is a plant with distinctive star-shaped yellow flowers. It grows in many places, including Europe, East Asia, and the Americas. It has been used as a health remedy since the 1st century AD.[lviii]

There is some evidence that St John's wort can treat mild insomnia, mild anxiety, and mild to moderate depression. Although it has been tested in some clinical trials, most health professionals classify it as an alternative medicine. Some studies have shown that it works as well as common prescription antidepressants. It's particularly effective for tiredness and the "on edge" feeling that sometimes comes with depression. However, it doesn't seem to work so well for severe forms of the illness.[lix]

You can buy it over the counter without a prescription in some countries, but that doesn't mean it is safe for everyone. If you are already taking medication, you must check with your doctor or pharmacist before trying it. Taking St. John's Wort with another antidepressant can lead to serotonin syndrome, where your body produces too much serotonin. In rare cases, this can cause fatal side effects. Follow the manufacturer's instructions carefully.

FOLATE

Folate is another name for vitamin B9, a water-soluble vitamin that helps build and maintain a healthy nervous system. This is why pregnant women and women trying to conceive should take folic acid, which is a manufactured version of folate. Low folate levels have been linked to depression,[lx] so taking folic acid could be a good idea if you struggle with low mood. It's safe for most people, and it is easy to buy over the counter, but check with your doctor or pharmacist before trying any supplement.

ZINC

People with mental health problems, particularly depression and anxiety, are more likely than the general population to be deficient in zinc.[lxi,lxii] As yet, no one knows why, but eating zinc-rich foods on a regular basis or taking a supplement might be a good idea. Fortified breakfast cereals, beef, pork, peas, cashews, pumpkin seeds, yogurt, lobster, chickpeas, oatmeal, almonds, and kidney beans are all sources of zinc.

SUMMARY

- There is no complementary treatment that will cure or treat BPD, but some people find that alternative medicine, supplements, and certain practices help relieve depression and anxiety.
- Massage, yoga, and aromatherapy can be very relaxing.
- There is some evidence that supplements, such as zinc and St John's Wort, can be helpful.
- If you want to try alternative or herbal medicine, always clear it with your doctor first. This is especially important if you are taking any other medications or supplements.

CHAPTER 7:

HOW TO HANDLE EXTREME EMOTIONS

I f you have BPD, you know that mood swings and fluctuating emotions can interfere with your daily life. Battling sadness, anger, frustration, and self-destructive impulses is exhausting. In this chapter, you'll learn how to deal with severe mood swings and keep yourself on an even keel.

WHAT IS EMOTION REGULATION, AND WHY DO YOU NEED TO MASTER IT?

Emotion regulation is a set of skills. They're important for everyone but particularly useful for people with BPD.

When you successfully regulate your emotions, you:[lxiii]

1. **Accept and understand your own feelings.**

    This means acknowledging your feelings, labeling them, and working out what triggered them. When they begin treatment, some people with BPD have no idea how to put their feelings into words. Some feel as though they have no emotions at all. Slowing down, pausing, and taking the time to label an emotion is the first step to getting past it.

2. **Draw on healthy coping skills that let you tolerate or "sit with" difficult emotions until they pass.**

   Using unhealthy coping strategies, such as self-injury and abusing substances, can put you and other people in danger. This chapter focuses on healthy coping skills. Swapping your old coping strategies for new behaviors takes a lot of practice, but it can be done.

3. **Control your behavior.**

   This means resisting self-destructive impulses and treating others with respect, even when you are very angry or unhappy. By improving your coping skills, you will be less likely to hurt yourself or damage your relationships.

   Regulating your emotions isn't about becoming hyper-rational or robotic. You've probably met people who seem to attract others to them by being kind, even-tempered, and upbeat. These people manage their emotions and avoid lashing out, but they are not boring. You can join them!

Exercise: How Well Do You Regulate Your Emotions?

Think back to the last time you had an extreme emotional reaction or a dramatic mood swing. What triggered it? How did you feel at the time? What strategies, if any, did you use to regulate your emotions?

Here are a few strategies to try the next time you feel your mood spiraling out of control:

1. **Give yourself permission to have emotions.**

   It's OK to have emotions, even if they are scary and overwhelming. Remind yourself that your feelings don't make you a bad person. For example, if you feel extremely angry at someone and want to punch them, this doesn't mean you should be ashamed; it only matters if you act on your impulses and hurt yourself or another person.

No one is perfect. Everyone has bad days; it's just that people with BPD tend to have more extreme emotions, more often. Remember, you are not the only one with this problem. Self-validation is important if you have BPD. You probably grew up with people who belittled your feelings. As an adult, you need to learn that it's OK to have emotions.

2. **Set a timer.**

Strong emotions and harmful urges tend to peak within 10 minutes. The next time you feel overwhelmed, set a timer. Sit or stand in the same place and just wait it out. If 10 minutes feels unrealistic, try 5 minutes or 3 minutes. As you wait for the clock to wind down, accept whatever thoughts and sensations arise in your mind and body. Remind yourself that no feeling, however strong, is forever.

3. **Use music therapy.**

If you can't bring yourself to turn on some happy music straight away, try the "match and switch" technique. Start with a couple of songs that reflect your mood, then put on a relaxing or upbeat track. Put together a playlist that reminds you of happier times. If you aren't in the mood for music, try a soundscape instead. White noise or recordings of natural sounds are soothing. There are lots of free videos available online.

4. **If you are a spiritual person, pray to God or the universe.**

   Some people find that saying a prayer gives them a sense of hope or renews their sense of purpose. If you believe in a higher power, ask them to help you stay with the emotion until it has run its course.

5. **Ground yourself using your senses.**

   What can you see, hear, smell, and touch? Pay close attention to your surroundings. This is a simple technique called grounding. As well as keeping you in the present moment, grounding is also a useful tool if you tend to dissociate under stress.

6. **Help someone else.**

   Being kind and helpful gives you a sense of purpose and improves your relationships. If you want to go one step further, offer to run an errand for someone. You don't have to tell them why you want to help out, just do it.

7. **Use progressive muscle relaxation.**

   Progressive muscle relaxation (PMR) involves tensing and releasing all the major muscle groups in your body. Sit or lie down somewhere comfortable. Bring your attention to your feet. As you breathe in, tense your toes and muscles in your feet as hard as you can. Hold for several seconds. As you exhale, release them. Work upwards, tensing your calves, thighs, buttocks, stomach, hands, forearms, shoulders, and face in turn. Be careful if you have any recent injuries.

8. **Mindful breathing.**

   Breathing exercises sound almost too simple to work, but they are effective when done properly. The key is to pay close attention to your breathing. As you count, notice how your lungs feel as air enters and leaves your body. Imagine that you are inhaling calming blue air and exhaling stale brown or gray energy you no longer want or need in your body. Breathe in for five seconds, then out for seven.

Mindfulness is a useful tool for anyone with BPD. By staying in the present, you can avoid over-analyzing your thoughts and feelings. In the next chapter, you'll learn how to use mindfulness techniques to regulate your emotions, cope with stress, and make better decisions.

9. **Write about your problems.**

Don't worry about whether your writing makes sense; just give yourself permission to vent. You can write in bullet points or jot down a list of words. If you don't want to write, draw a picture. What does your feeling look like? Is it a monster, an animal, a symbol, or a color? When you've finished venting, rip up the paper or burn it.

10. **Calm your nervous system with cold water.**

Submerge your face in icy cold water or put an ice pack on your face for 30 seconds. These techniques trigger your mammalian diving reflex, which kickstarts your parasympathetic nervous system (PNS). You will feel calmer within seconds. Make sure you cool down the area immediately beneath your eyes and above your cheekbones.[lxiv]

If you have a heart condition or circulatory problem, don't use this technique without checking with your doctor first because it temporarily slows down your heartbeat.

11. Do 5-10 minutes of intense exercise.

Do some jumping jacks, a few push-ups, or run in place. When you work out, your body produces endorphins. These chemicals quickly elevate your mood. Exercise lowers your levels of cortisol and adrenaline, which both cause jittery feelings and prime your body for a "fight or flight" response.

12. Call a helpline.

The National Alliance on Mental Illness (NAMI) has a crisis text service, the Crisis Text Line. You can access it by texting NAMI to 741-741. It offers support every hour of every day. If you are having thoughts of suicide, call 1 (800) 273-TALK to speak to Samaritans USA, a suicide prevention charity. Most countries have crisis lines, but you'll need to do a little Google research to find them. Research a few numbers when you feel stable, and be sure to add them to your phone contacts.

13. Spend time with a pet.

A pet offers companionship and affection. Animals do not judge or give unwanted advice. Lots of people find it easier to talk to their pets than they do to humans.

14. Use opposite action

To use opposite action is to deliberately act against a destructive urge or emotion. This is a tricky skill to develop. It takes practice and determination to confront your feelings and decide on an opposite action.

Here are some examples of what it looks like in practice:

Problem: You feel completely demotivated and can't find the energy to do anything.

Opposite action: Make a realistic to-do list and work your way through it. Focus on one thing at a time.

Problem: You want to try a new activity, but you are so afraid of failing that you can't seem to get started.

Opposite action: Commit to starting anyway. Tell yourself that it's normal and OK to worry that you won't be good enough and that fearing failure doesn't mean you won't be able to do a task or meet a goal.

Problem: You want to withdraw from your friends and family. Socializing feels like an impossible task.

Opposite action: Write a light-hearted message to someone and send it. Ask them what they've been doing lately. If they respond positively, take it one step further and ask if you can meet up or talk on the phone. Whatever response you get (or don't get), give yourself lots of praise for reaching out.

Problem: You feel guilty for something you've done or said.

Opposite action: If it's based in fact—i.e., you really have hurt someone—guilt can be useful. It's a sign that you've done something that doesn't align with your values. If you can apologize to the person you've hurt, do so. If your guilt is irrational, change your body language. Act as though you accept yourself. Sit or stand up straight, remind yourself of your good points, and gently redirect yourself to your next activity.

These strategies won't work for everyone. You'll need to experiment to find out what makes you feel better. Therapists and doctors can steer you in the right direction and give you coping skills to try, but you need to take responsibility for handling your feelings.

Exercise: Making A Personal Action Plan

As you become more skilled in dealing with your emotions, you can start putting together a list of techniques that have worked for you. Every time you use one of these skills successfully, make a note of it. In time, you'll build a list you can refer to whenever you start feeling overwhelmed.

HANDLING EMPTINESS

An absence of emotion can be just as difficult to deal with as dramatic feelings. It's scary to feel detached, numb, or indifferent. Some people with BPD describe their emptiness as a void; it feels like whatever you do, nothing will fill it. You need to learn to tolerate emptiness. Otherwise, you'll continually look for distractions—and some distractions, such as rocky relationships or addictive behaviors, can make things worse.

Adopt an attitude of gentle curiosity. Feeling this way doesn't make you a bad or flawed person. It just means you are going through a difficult time. Do some detective work. Emptiness can be a psychological defense against an unpleasant emotion you'd rather avoid.

People with BPD are often taught that their reactions to events and situations are somehow wrong. In time, they learn it is safer to shut down their emotions altogether than to actively participate in life and welcome any and all feelings. Try to identify your triggers. If you find yourself feeling particularly empty all of a sudden, what were you doing or thinking about immediately before that feeling set in?

Some people "numb out" when they feel overwhelmed by responsibility. Is it time to overhaul your to-do list or tackle a task you've been putting off? Break chores, assignments, and projects down into small subtasks. If you aren't sure where to start, is there anyone you could ask for help?

WHY LEARNING TO MANAGE YOUR FEELINGS HELPS WITH DISSOCIATION

Some mental health professionals think that dissociation is a protective mechanism. Dissociating from a situation means you don't have to think about it or confront your feelings. Unfortunately, although it can temporarily shield you from uncomfortable emotions, dissociation also robs you of good feelings. Another problem is that it makes you more likely to take risks because you feel detached from the world and yourself.[lxv]

By using the techniques in this book, you will start to dissociate less often. When you learn to acknowledge, work with, and express your feelings, your brain won't need to dissociate as a coping mechanism. Grounding and mindfulness exercises are especially useful for this problem.

COPING WITH SHAME

Shame is a hallmark of BPD. It's linked to a general sense of self-loathing and self-disgust. Why? One theory is that shame is a side effect of childhood abuse, and people with BPD are more likely to have been abused at a young age than the rest of the population. Children and young people don't always understand that their abuser deserves to feel ashamed and guilty. Instead, they may assume that something about them invited the abuse.

On the other hand, research shows that people with both BPD and post-traumatic stress disorder (PTSD) don't feel more shame than those with BPD alone.[lxvi] Shame might be common in BPD because sufferers grew up in invalidating environments where normal and healthy emotions and behaviors were punished. As adults, they live in a constant state of shame, assuming that everything they say, do, or even think is somehow wrong.

There is a difference between guilt and shame. To feel guilty is to feel as though you have done something wrong. For example, if you drive too quickly in a fit of temper and cause an accident, you might feel guilty because you know you should not have broken the speed limit. Guilt often goes hand in hand with embarrassment if others find out what we've done. Humans crave approval and knowing that we have broken social norms or rules can leave us feeling exposed or humiliated. Shame goes deeper. It is the sense of "being" wrong, rather than merely "doing" wrong.

QUESTIONS TO HELP YOU EXPLORE SHAME

There is no magic cure for shame. But asking yourself the following questions and thinking or journaling about the answers might help.

Exercise: Exploring Shame

1. *Where did the shame come from?*
2. *Did anyone from your past make you feel inferior, belittle you, or blame you for things that were not your fault?*
3. *If you've done something that makes you feel guilty or ashamed, try to uncover your motives without judging yourself.*
4. *Commit to judging other people less often. In accepting others, you are more likely to accept yourself.*

A NOTE ABOUT TRAUMA

Shame can have roots in trauma. Trauma therapy is a complicated topic that is beyond the scope of this book, and it is hard
to do by yourself. If you have experienced traumatic events,
whether recently or in the distant past, you will probably need
professional help to move past it.

SUMMARY

- Extreme emotions and mood swings are part of life with
  BPD.
- Learning to regulate your emotions takes time, but it
  pays off.
- Giving yourself permission to have strong feelings is the
  first step in managing them.
- There are numerous techniques you can use to calm
  down, so you don't get swept away by your emotions.
- Not all self-care or self-help techniques will work for
  everyone, and they may only work some of the time.
- Shame is a hallmark of BPD and can be crippling, but
  like other difficult emotions, you can learn how to deal
  with it.

CHAPTER 8:

HOW TO USE MINDFULNESS TO COPE WITH BPD SYMPTOMS

In the previous chapter, you picked up some coping skills that can help you deal with unpleasant emotions. We're now going to look at a skill that deserves a chapter of its own: mindfulness.

WHAT IS MINDFULNESS?

When was the last time you lived fully in the moment? So many of us are preoccupied with thoughts and worries about the past and future. It's sensible to make plans, and sometimes it's smart to dwell on the past—it can teach us some useful lessons. But if you can't ground yourself in the here and now, you'll be stressed, unhappy, and waste a lot of time dwelling on things that may or may not happen.

Mindfulness isn't a single technique, but rather an approach to life. This is how Jon Kabat-Zinn, a much-respected mindfulness expert, defines it:

"Paying attention in a particular way: on purpose, in the present moment, and nonjudgmentally."[lxvii]

Some people use "mindfulness" interchangeably with

"meditation," but they are not the same. Although they can both calm you down and silence a busy mind, there are a couple of differences.

Exercise: Where Is Your Mind Right Now?

When you've finished reading this paragraph, put this book down for three minutes. Sit quietly and observe your mind. What are you thinking and feeling? Is your mind focused and tranquil, like a smooth pond, or is it flitting from thought to thought? Our minds are rarely still; it's quite astonishing how busy they are! Congratulations—you've completed your first simple mindfulness exercise.

MINDFULNESS VERSUS MEDITATION

While mindfulness is a state of intentional awareness, meditation is usually based around a formal practice. When meditating, a person might use mantras or sounds to channel their focus and prevent their mind from wandering.

Some people use meditation as a broad term that refers to various practices, traditionally associated with ancient religions, that help someone move to a higher level of consciousness or enlightenment. This includes yoga, observing a state of silence, breathing exercises, and mindfulness.

In summary, meditation can be a form of mindfulness, but not all mindfulness involves meditation. Unlike meditation, you can practice mindfulness absolutely anywhere.

WHY IS MINDFULNESS SO EFFECTIVE FOR PEOPLE WITH BPD?

Mindful people have fewer BPD symptoms, and mindfulness is great for anyone in recovery.[lxviii] Why?

MINDFUL PEOPLE ARE BETTER THAN NON-MINDFUL PEOPLE AT REGULATING THEIR EMOTIONS.

Mindful people recognize and accept their feelings and events that are unfolding around them. This puts them in a good position to think clearly about what is happening and react appropriately. They know that everyone's emotions come and go, and that having unpleasant and less socially desirable feeling like anger and anxiety, don't make them bad or inferior people. In other words, they don't judge themselves on the basis of how they think or feel, as people with BPD tend to do.

MINDFUL PEOPLE DON'T AVOID OR OVERREACT TO DIFFICULT SITUATIONS AND EMOTIONS.

Some people with BPD decide that relationships, jobs, and other parts of everyday life are too overwhelming. Believing that they can't cope, they try to avoid the outside world altogether. The trouble with this strategy is that the more you avoid the outside world, the less prepared you are to deal with setbacks and unpleasant emotions. What's more, shutting yourself off from everyone and everything else will make you lonely and depressed.

STAYING MINDFUL HELPS WITH BUILDING AND MAINTAINING HEALTHY RELATIONSHIPS.

If you overreact to any insult or criticism—even if it's mild—your relationships will not last long. The other person will feel as though they are walking on eggshells around you. When you can pause to think about how someone else is thinking and feeling, it's easier to get your responses under control. Staying mindful gives you some breathing space.

Mindfulness Helps Reduce Destructive and Impulsive Behaviors.

Learning to tolerate distress in yourself and other people means you don't have to rely on destructive coping mechanisms such as binge eating, self-injury, or compulsive shopping. Trying to stop this kind of behavior using willpower alone is exhausting and not very effective. Sitting with emotions until they naturally ebb away, staying mindful, and using the kind of healthy coping mechanisms in the previous chapter are better approaches.

Mindfulness is Empowering.

When you are no longer afraid of your own feelings, you'll be better equipped to handle challenging situations. This gives you more options. For example, if you haven't been able to work because taking criticism is impossible for you to bear, learning how to be mindful and tolerate your feelings could open up the possibility of getting back into work.

If you've been stuck in patterns of unhelpful behaviors for years, you'd be forgiven for thinking that you'll never break free. But there is every reason to stay hopeful. Your brain, just like everyone else's, is flexible. In simple terms, by deliberately changing your behavior and the way you think, you can "rewire" your brain and develop new, healthier patterns.

Mindfulness Helps You Get the Most Out of Therapy.

Therapy is easier when you stay mindful and self-aware. Talking to a therapist or other people in a group involves sharing memories and thoughts with someone else, which can trigger difficult emotions. If you can draw on your mindfulness skills in these moments, you will stay grounded. You'll be in a good place to take a careful look at your thoughts and feelings.

HOW MINDFULNESS CHANGES YOUR BRAIN

As you learned earlier in this book, those with BPD have brains that work a bit differently from most people. Some areas are more or less responsive than usual, and these differences make emotional regulation and rational thought more difficult.

Regular mindfulness helps the prefrontal cortex (PFC), a part of the brain that helps you make smart decisions, plan for the future, and function properly. Mindfulness also reduces activity in the amygdala, an area in the brain that triggers emotional responses.

MINDFULNESS EXERCISES TO TRY:

1. **Mindful eating**

    Because eating requires all your senses and you do it several times per day, it's a great way to start experimenting with mindfulness. For this exercise, you need a small piece of food you can eat with your fingers, such as a grape, piece of chocolate, or cracker. As you eat, take the opportunity to tune into your five senses:

    Touch: What is the food's texture? Is it rough or smooth? Hot or cold?

    Sight: What color is the food? Is it shiny or dull?

    Smell: What does this food smell like? Is it subtle or strong?

Taste: Take a bit of food and roll it slowly around your mouth. How would you describe the taste? Is it sweet, salty, sour, bitter, or a combination?

Sound: As you bite into the food, what noise does it make? Is a "quiet" or "loud" food?

Binge eating is a common impulsive behavior in people with BPD. Mindful eating can help you slow down, eat less, and relearn to enjoy your meals.

2. **Mindful breathing**[lxix]
    We take breathing for granted. When was the last time you slowed down and appreciated your lungs for keeping you alive?

    To practice mindful breathing, sit or lie down somewhere comfortable. If you can't find a chair or bed, you can do it while standing. You can do this exercise with your eyes open or closed.

    Spend a few seconds observing your body. How does it feel—light, heavy, tense, or relaxed? Feel the weight of your body against the chair or bed. If you are standing up, feel your feet on the ground. Next, tune into your breathing. Inhale for 3 seconds, hold for 2 seconds, then exhale slowly for 4 seconds. Try to do this for 7 minutes, but don't worry if that seems unmanageable right now. Two or three minutes is better than nothing.

    Notice how your chest rises and falls when you breathe in and out. How do your nostrils, throat, chest, and abdomen feel?

3. **Mindful walking**[lxx]

Like breathing, most of us don't think much about how we walk, but walking is a perfect opportunity to practice mindfulness. Try doing this exercise outside in the fresh air; it's a good way to clear your head. If you can't get outside, you can do this exercise indoors as long as you have a few meters of clear floor space.

Start by paying attention to how your body feels and moves when you take a step. Are you swaying side to side? How does your foot feel when it makes contact with the floor? Are your arms loose and relaxed or tense? What about your hands?

Next, tune into your other senses. What can you see, hear, or smell? If any judgment comes up, like "I hate that smell!" notice them and let them go. Your aim is to stay in the present moment. At the end of your walk—aim for 10 minutes—stop and reflect how it felt to be mindful. Try to carry this state of mind with you for the rest of the day.

4. **Mindful showering**

Next time you are in the shower, pay attention to the feel of water against your skin. Is it cool, warm, or hot? Is the shower gentle or high pressure? Vary the temperature slightly. Squeeze some shower gel onto your palm and make a lather. Inhale the scent of the gel. Feel the bubbles between your fingers and between your palms. Slowly rub the foam into your skin.

Challenge yourself to practice mindfulness for a few minutes every day. You'll find it frustrating at first. Your mind will wander. That's OK. Mindfulness is a skill.

Within a few days, it will start to get easier. The exercises in this chapter are a good way to get started if you like step-by-step instructions, but mindfulness is an attitude, not an action.

WORKING WITH FEELINGS MINDFULLY

Taking a mindful approach to unpleasant thoughts and feelings is to acknowledge them, watch them, and let them go. Some mindfulness practitioners compare the mind to the sky, and thoughts and feelings to clouds.

Just as clouds drift across the sky, float away, and disperse, our inner states are fleeting. If they are simply allowed to exist, they will fade and drift away of their own accord. There is no way to force the clouds in the sky to move on, and trying to push them away is futile. The same principle applies to feelings. Trying to wish them away using willpower alone doesn't work.

When you next spiral into an intense emotional state, observe what is going on in your body and mind. Is your body showing tell-tale signs of stress, like muscle tension, sweating, or heavy breathing? Is your mind racing faster than usual? Is your inner voice louder? Are you jumping to conclusions, judging someone without knowing the facts, or envisioning worst-case scenarios?

This kind of awareness is the first step toward working with destructive thought patterns, also known as cognitive distortions. In the next chapter, you'll learn how to identify the types of cognitive distortions that affect you, and how to both accept and challenge them.

Using mindfulness in difficult moments

The exercises in this chapter have two purposes. First, practicing them regularly gets you in the habit of mindfulness, which will then start to spill over into your everyday life. Second, you can also use them when you feel out of control or overwhelmed by strong emotions. For example, if you are feeling anxious at work, do a few minutes of mindful breathing. If you are feeling sad at home, you could take a mindful shower.

Mindfulness gives you a chance to step back from whatever is bothering you. Sometimes this is enough to make you feel better. Other times, you can combine it with the skills in the previous chapter.

Summary

- Mindfulness is an effective skill for managing BPD. You can use it alongside the other coping strategies in this book.
- To be mindful is to accept and live in the present moment.
- Regular mindfulness practice will make you a calmer, more resilient person. Within a few weeks, you will find it easier to regulate your emotions.
- Mindfulness is simple, but not easy. It requires regular practice.
- You can call on your mindfulness skills anywhere.

CHAPTER 9:

HOW TO TACKLE UNHELPFUL THOUGHTS

In the previous chapter, you learned how to use mindfulness techniques to detach yourself from difficult thoughts and feelings and wait for them to pass. However, if you want to break destructive patterns such as overreacting to minor problems or assuming that other people are out to get you, you need to go one step further. You need to not only accept your thoughts but also learn how and when to challenge them.

REFRAME YOUR THOUGHTS, CHANGE YOUR MOOD

When you begin to interpret situations and other people's actions in a more realistic way, it will become easier to make healthy choices and take care of yourself. This is the basic idea behind a type of therapy known as cognitive-behavioral therapy (CBT).

According to CBT practitioners, how we think about a situation dictates how we feel about it. Our interpretations of events can be more important than the event itself. For example, let's suppose your friend hasn't returned a text or call.

If you tell yourself, "Oh, my friend is probably busy, I hope we can catch up soon," you'll feel slightly disappointed. You might call or message another friend instead, or occupy yourself with something else. But if you say to yourself, "Typical! They don't care about me, no one does," you'll fall into a pit of self-loathing and loneliness. You probably won't feel like doing anything that could make you happy, and you might hesitate to reach out to other friends because you are convinced that you are unlikeable.

This is a simple example, but it shows how our thoughts influence our feelings, which in turn affect our actions. CBT therapists help clients understand these links and make positive changes. One key pillar of CBT is to challenge unhelpful thoughts. By teaching yourself new ways of thinking about yourself and the world, you can help yourself feel better.

We've already looked at the most popular treatments for BPD, including Dialectical Behavior Therapy (DBT) and Schema-Focused Therapy (SFT). Both of these approaches are based on CBT principles. This chapter contains some exercises based on CBT interventions. When used alongside mindfulness (which is at the core of DBT), they can transform how you see yourself, other people, and the world.

COGNITIVE DISTORTIONS

People with BPD, depression, anxiety, and other mental illnesses tend to use unhelpful styles and patterns of thinking. These patterns are called thinking errors or cognitive distortions. Identifying your cognitive distortions is a key step on the road to recovery. You will soon start to see how they affect your mood and why you must address them.

Let's look at the most common of these patterns and why they cause problems.

1. **Black and white thinking:** Seeing something or someone as completely good or bad. Black and white thinking can also take the form of "always" or "nothing" thoughts, such as "I've failed, I always fail!" or "She's always out to annoy me!" Your black and white thinking might be triggered by minor incidents, such as a partner calling you an hour later than they said they would.

   Why this is a problem: You can't have good relationships with others—or yourself—if you can't take a balanced view and accept that human beings are complicated. Sometimes they are wonderful, and sometimes they are annoying or unkind. You don't have to tolerate abusive behavior, but you need to appreciate that no one is completely perfect or terrible.

2. **Blaming:** Being quick to assign blame to someone without owning your role in a situation or taking responsibility for your feelings. For example, "It's my father's fault I have an anger problem!" and "It's my friend's fault I feel so bad because she started an argument!" are blaming statements.

   Why this is a problem: When you blame other people for your feelings, you are handing over your power. You are effectively saying to yourself, "I can't control my emotions, and I'm at the mercy of others." This attitude will make you feel helpless. The truth is that no one can "make" you feel a particular way. As the example earlier in this chapter shows, your interpretation of events makes all the difference.

3. **Filtering:** Focusing on the negative aspects or down-sides of a situation. For people who filter, the glass is always half empty rather than half full. For example, a teacher who spends a lot of time thinking about the one child who doesn't seem to be enjoying their class, rather than the rest who engage well with the work, is filtering.

   Why this is a problem: Dwelling on unpleasant details and minor mistakes makes it hard to take a healthy pride in your achievements. It stops you from appreciating what has gone well, which in turn stunts your self-esteem.

4. **Mind reading:** The assumption that you can know what someone else is thinking. As you can imagine, this causes major problems in relationships. For example, someone who says things like "I just know that she thinks I'm stupid!" or "He's out to get me, I know it," is mind reading. Some therapists call this distortion "jumping to conclusions" or "fortune telling."[lxxi]

   Why this is a problem: Healthy relationships are based on communication and trust, not assumptions and spurious conclusions.

5. **Catastrophizing:** Leaping to the worst-case scenario. The phrase "making mountains out of molehills" sums up this cognitive distortion. For example, suppose you are running late for work one morning. It would be perfectly reasonable to feel slightly annoyed with yourself and to worry about being late.

   However, if you are prone to catastrophizing, you might assume that your day is ruined, that your boss will be mad, that you will lose your job, and you'll lose your home. In most cases, this would be a disproportional reaction.

Why this is a problem: People who blow everything out of proportion go from crisis to crisis. They are in a state of chronic stress. For those with BPD, this stress can make their other symptoms, especially emotional dysregulation and paranoid ideation, worse.

6.   **"Shoulding:"** Whenever you use the words "should," "must," and "ought," there's a good chance you are judging yourself and others in a way that sets you up to feel disappointed. Shoulding often comes packaged with unreasonably high expectations. For example, you might tell yourself that you should always be nice and kind to people, even if they treat you badly. Or you may think that everyone else must treat you well.

Why this is a problem: Judgmental people are not attractive and don't have many friends. Even if you don't speak badly of someone to their face, they will soon realize that you are capable of judging them behind their back. In addition, judging yourself doesn't feel good. It erodes your self-esteem and can make you depressed and anxious.

7.   **Emotional reasoning:** Do you assume that if you feel something is the case, then it must be true? This is called emotional reasoning. Common examples include "I feel like a bad person, so I must be" and "This feels scary, so it must be bad and dangerous."

Why this is a problem: Emotions are a normal, healthy part of life. But if you rely too heavily on emotional reasoning, you won't make good decisions. For example, if you assume that you are a boring person just because you happen to feel that way, you'll miss out on chances to make new friends. Or if you feel like a bad person and accept this feeling as truth, you are more likely to act on impulses to hurt yourself because you feel as though you deserve it.

8. **Control fallacies:** They come in two forms. The first one is a fallacy of external control, in which you believe external circumstances are completely to blame for your behavior. For example, you might say, "It's not my fault that I can't make friends; my parents didn't teach me social skills."

   The second form is the fallacy of internal control, in which you assume that you alone are responsible for other people's feelings and happiness. For instance, you might think things like "They seem angry today. I bet it's because of something I did."

   Why this is a problem: These fallacies stop you from owning your role in a situation, learning from your mistakes, and taking responsibility for your personal growth.

9. **Fallacy of fairness/heaven's reward fallacy:** This involves the notion that self-sacrifice is always rewarded, that hard work will pay off, and noble efforts always will be recognized.

   Why this is a problem: The world is not a fair place. Holding onto a belief in a just world leaves you vulnerable to disappointment. If you insist that you should get a reward for doing the right thing, you'll quickly become discouraged, because the world does not work this way.

Exercise: What Cognitive Distortions Do You Use?

As you read through the list of distortions, did any jump out at you? Try keeping a cognitive distortion log for a couple of days. Every time you have a negative mood swing, ask yourself what you were thinking immediately before it happened. Were you using any of these thinking errors?

THE NEXT STEP: OVERCOMING THINKING ERRORS

Identifying your cognitive distortions is the first step to changing them. Here's what to do next:

1. **Weigh up the evidence.**
   What is the evidence for and against the thought? If you are caught up in your emotions and finding it hard to think clearly, use some of the coping strategies from previous chapters first. Pretend that you are helping someone else gain perspective on the situation. This can help you detach yourself and see things more clearly.

2. **Ask yourself what you would say to a loved one.**
   We are often harsher on ourselves than we are with others. Pretend you are your own best friend for a moment. How would you talk to them?

   For example, let's say your friend failed an exam and labeled themselves stupid. You wouldn't agree with your friend that because they *feel* stupid, they must be unintelligent. You would encourage them instead, pointing out their past successes. You might also suggest that their way of looking at the situation is not helpful.

3. Re-evaluate your language.

Psychologist John Grohol points out that when making harsh judgments about ourselves or others, we tend to use labels that are neither clear nor helpful. Challenging the terms you are using can diffuse a thought.[lxxii]

For example, if you have made a mistake at work and are calling yourself an idiot, think about what this really means. Is there a universal, clear consensus of what it means to be an idiot? What does it mean to say you are an idiot at work, at home, or in a relationship? If someone is an idiot, have they always been that way? Is it possible to be an idiot 100% of the time? Dwell on these questions for a few minutes. You'll get some distance from your thoughts, and you'll start to realize that this kind of labeling is pointless.

4. Embrace the scientific method.

Is there anything you can do to test your thought? Pretend you are a scientist. Set up an experiment that will help you discover whether your thought is true. For example, suppose you have had an argument with your partner and are having the thought, "I can't get along with anyone!" You could test this thought by calling or messaging a friend or relative and having a pleasant conversation, thereby proving to yourself that even though you had a fight with your partner, you are perfectly able to communicate with other people.

5. **Reassign responsibility.**

   Do you assign yourself too much blame? Try the responsibility pie technique to gain a new perspective. Draw a circle on a piece of paper. This is the responsibility pie. Divide it into slices, with the size of the slice reflecting the role you, other people, and external factors played in that situation. For instance, if you had a fight with your partner, the largest slice of the pie might belong to you, but it's likely they also played a part. This technique is also useful if you are too quick to blame others for everything that goes wrong.

6. **Ask yourself what someone you admire would say.**

   Just for a couple of minutes, pretend you are someone else—specifically, someone you admire. What would they say about the situation? What would they tell you?

7. **Think about the advantages and disadvantages of challenging your unhelpful thought.**

   If you need some motivation to use these techniques, do a cost-benefit analysis. What do you have to lose by trying them? How are your thinking errors holding you back, and what are the benefits of addressing them?

   Give these strategies a fair try. Some will only work with practice, and others may not work for you at all. That's OK. Although lots of people with BPD have similar problems, there isn't a "one size fits all" solution.

WHEN TO CHALLENGE YOUR THOUGHTS

You don't have to challenge every negative thought you have. That would be too time-consuming, and it isn't necessary. Your goal is to notice when your thinking errors are causing you to feel especially sad, angry, anxious, lonely, defeated, or unhappy, and then use the strategies in this chapter to reframe the situation. Try to practice your favorite techniques several times each day.

PARANOID THOUGHTS

Paranoid thoughts occur on a spectrum, from mild to severe. On the milder end, you may know that your thoughts are unreasonable, yet still be unable to shake them off. If you are suffering from severe paranoia, you may lose all insight and sincerely believe that others are out to harm you. (Note that if you are in the grip of severe paranoia, it is unlikely you would have enough insight to realize something is wrong and would not be reading this chapter.)

There are a couple of self-help strategies that can help with mild paranoia.[lxxiii] First, you can make a decision to give someone the benefit of the doubt. Consider other explanations behind someone's actions. For instance, let's say your colleagues have started spending more time with one another outside of work and haven't invited you. You have a suspicion that they hate you and are plotting to have you fired from your job.

But could there be another explanation? For example, it's possible they think you are shy and reserved, so have not invited you along because they assume you would turn them down. Or perhaps they are rude and inconsiderate, but that doesn't mean they are actively conspiring to get rid of you.

Second, you can decide that even if your suspicions are true, you aren't going to launch an attack in retaliation. Someone may or may not be insulting or undermining you, but you have the power to choose how to respond. Making a decision to avoid retaliation unless absolutely necessary (for example, in physical self-defense) can bring you some peace of mind.

If you are prone to paranoia, the best long-term strategy is to work on your stress management skills. Because people with BPD are more likely to suffer from paranoid thoughts when under pressure, emotional regulation skills are the best defense.

SUMMARY

- Cognitive distortions, including catastrophizing and jumping to conclusions, underpin many of the troubling thoughts and feelings in people with BPD.
- By challenging your unhelpful thoughts, you can learn to see situations in a more balanced way.
- Learning about cognitive distortions will help you understand how your thoughts are making you unhappy.
- The first step is to identify your thinking errors. You can then use several strategies to tackle them.
- Severe paranoia requires professional help, but you can cope with mild paranoia by deciding to give people the benefit of the doubt and to avoid retaliation unless necessary.

CHAPTER 10:

HOW TO HAVE HEALTHY RELATIONSHIPS WHEN YOU HAVE BPD

Efforts to avoid real or perceived abandonment and intense, unstable relationships are two of the BPD criteria listed in the DSM. Although it's possible to have a BPD diagnosis without relationship problems, most people with BPD find it difficult to get along with others. In this chapter, you'll pick up some skills that will help you start and maintain satisfying relationships.

INTERPERSONAL EFFECTIVENESS—THE KEY TO MAKING AND KEEPING FRIENDS

Do you know someone who is comfortable around others, knows how to build stable, healthy relationships, and is generally at ease in social situations? Psychologists describe such people as interpersonally effective.

Interpersonally effective people know what they want from their relationships and interactions with others, and they know how to ask for it. For instance, if they want to ask a friend for a favor, they know how to balance their own needs with their friends' wishes. They know how to stay true to their own values, how to keep a relationship going, and how to resolve arguments. They know their own worth and maintain a healthy level of self-respect.

We're going to look at several communication skills that will improve your interpersonal effectiveness. It's important that you use the other skills in this book too; keeping your emotions under control and challenging your irrational thoughts are also essential if you want strong, steady relationships.

SKILLS YOU NEED:

Skill #1: "I feel..." statements

When you want someone to change their behavior, avoid using generalized emotive statements that begin with "You," such as "You never think of me." Instead, begin by saying how you feel, why you feel that way, and what you would like to happen instead. Try to think of a practical way you could solve the problem and present it as a suggestion.

For example, instead of saying, "You never do any of the housework! You treat me like a servant, and it makes me mad!" you could say, "I feel as though you take me for granted when you leave all the chores to me. I would like us to set aside a time to draw up a chore rotation, so the workload is distributed fairly."

Exercise: Using "I" statements

Think about a problem that is currently bothering you in a close relationship. How could you use "I" statements to start a constructive discussion?

Skill #2: Saying "no"

If you are desperate for others to like you—and many people with BPD are keen to impress others in a bid to win their affections—saying "no" isn't easy. But saying "no" is a vital skill in upholding boundaries and keeping your self-respect. Sometimes people will ask you to do things that go against your personal values and goals. It's up to you to draw some lines.

Rehearse a few ways of saying "no." Prepare some phrases you can use the next time you need to turn someone down.

For example:

> "No, thank you, but I appreciate the offer."
> "That doesn't work for me. No, thank you."
> "That's kind of you to think of me, but I'm going to pass."

If someone doesn't respect your "no," repeat it in exactly the same tone of voice until they accept it. This is called the broken record technique.

Some people are slow to respect boundaries. If you can't avoid the person, you will need to spell out the consequences and then follow through. For example, suppose your friend is trying to convince you to go out, but you are tired and would rather stay in. They do not respect your "no," and keep pushing you to change your mind.

In this situation, you could say, "If you don't stop asking me to go out drinking with you, I'm going to end this conversation and hang up the phone." For people with BPD who are afraid of rejection, this is a tough skill to master. But in the end, people who do not respect your boundaries are not the kind of people you need in your life.

Skill #3: Active listening

Few people know how to listen effectively, but it's key to understanding another person's perspective, which in turn is the foundation of mutual understanding and healthy compromise.

Remember to SHUSH:[lxxiv]

Show you care: Put down your phone and give the other person your full attention. Make eye contact, lean forward slightly, and nod whenever they finish making a point.

Have patience: Some people are more longwinded than others. Give them time to get to the point, especially if you are having a sensitive discussion. When someone pauses, count to three slowly in your head before responding. They may want to expand on what they've just said.

Use open questions: If you want to learn more about someone's point of view or experiences, use questions that invite a longer answer than "yes" or "no." For example: "How did that make you feel?" and "What happened after that?" are open questions.

Say it back: When the other person has finished making a point, summarize what they've said in your own words to make sure you have understood. Give them the chance to correct you if you've misunderstood. For example, if they seem mad because someone has lied to them, you could say something like, "Going by what you've told me, you're angry at the situation because you weren't told the truth. Have I got that right?"

Have courage: Having a meaningful conversation or an exchange of views, especially if you're talking about personal or sensitive issues, is not easy. Be prepared to clarify any misunderstandings if they come up. If someone clams up or doesn't want to go into detail about a topic, do not take it personally.

Exercise: Practice Your SHUSH Skills

The next time you have a conversation—whether it's casual or serious—use the SHUSH technique. It's OK if you can't remember all the steps. This takes practice! Evaluate your efforts. Did you learn something about the other person? Did they respond more positively to you than usual?

Skill #4: Dealing with the urge to "out" someone

Telling tales on a friend or partner is destructive behavior, but stopping isn't a simple matter of willpower. The best way to stop 'tattling' is to take a holistic approach to recovery. Learning to regulate your emotions, manage your stress levels, and overcome thinking errors will naturally reduce the urge to destroy confidences and reveal someone else's secrets.

However, there are also a couple of things you can do in the moment when you feel yourself devaluing someone. Treat a tattling episode as an anxiety attack. Deep breathing and mindfulness can help you feel less overwhelmed and gain a better perspective on the situation. Use grounding exercises to distract you from racing thoughts and anxieties. Wherever you are, pause and tune into your senses. What can you see, hear, touch, smell, and feel?

Try to identify triggers and warning signs. For example, if you find yourself using words that indicate black and white thinking, like "never," "always," "none," and "all," you may be about to rat on someone or something. Keep a "gossiping diary" to help you uncover triggers.

Skill #5: Owning your mistake

In a healthy relationship, both people acknowledge that they are capable of making mistakes. Even people with excellent communication skills will occasionally hurt their loved ones because no one can be completely understanding and accepting all of the time. Disagreements and friction are inevitable.

Fortunately, owning your mistakes, learning from them, and making sincere apologies where appropriate can repair damaged relationships. When someone tells you that your actions have hurt them, try not to get defensive. Use the listening skills above to learn how they feel about the situation. Remind yourself that conflict and misunderstandings are normal in relationships, and the other person won't necessarily abandon you or cut you out of their lives.

If you need to apologize, use this formula:

1. **Start by acknowledging what you did.** For example, "I realize I was rude to you and called you names."

2. **Acknowledge how it made them feel.** For example, "I know it made you feel belittled and angry."

3. **Express regret.** For example, "I am very sorry. I should not have said those things."

4. **Say what you will do differently in the future.** For example, "I will be more mindful of my language in the future, and I'll work on staying calm when our conversations get heated."

It's then up to the other person to decide whether to accept your apology. You don't have a right to forgiveness. Do not offer pseudo-apologies like "I'm sorry you feel that way" or "It's a shame you got upset." Fake apologies are passive-aggressive and will only make the situation worse.

Skill #6: Keeping your focus

Do you tend to drag up the past or go off on a tangent when working out an issue with a friend or partner? If you notice an urge to bring up something that happened a long time ago, pause and ask yourself whether raising it will move the conversation forward.

There's nothing wrong with making a few notes to prepare for a serious discussion with someone. Just like office meetings have agendas, you can set out your main points in advance.

Skill #7: Aim for a resolution, not a victory

Winning an argument or forcing someone else is satisfying in the moment, but this kind of attitude isn't good for your relationships. Aim to cooperate and compromise with someone, even if you don't like them. You can push for someone to admit they are wrong, but at what cost? You might feel triumphant for a few minutes, but your relationship will suffer. When someone else senses you are only out to win rather than come to an agreement, they may get defensive or hostile.

Skill #8: Know when to take a break

When we get stressed, the areas of our brain responsible for forward planning and emotion regulation shut down. That's why it's hard to think clearly when you feel very angry, upset, or anxious.

Taking five or ten minutes away from a heated argument can give you a new perspective and stop you from saying something you'll regret later. Tell the other person that you're going to take a few minutes to cool off. They might appreciate the break too.

Skill #9: Stop mind reading

When you learn how to communicate with others by developing interpersonal effectiveness skills, you won't have to guess what they are thinking—you can ask instead! Mind reading fuels paranoia. If you sincerely believe that someone is thinking negative things about you, it's hard to trust them.

The next time you get angry or upset with someone, stop and take a few deep breaths. Ask yourself, "What assumptions am I making here?" Even if you know the person well, you still have no way of knowing exactly what they are thinking. You also need to accept that no one owes you a detailed account of their thoughts.

Skill #10: Take responsibility for your own feelings.

Do you catch yourself saying things like, "You always make me angry!" or "She makes me feel crazy"? By deciding that someone else "makes" you feel a certain way, you are handing over your power. As hard as it is to believe sometimes, no one has the ability to make you feel any particular way. What someone says or does is an external event. As you know from previous chapters, how you interpret an external event ultimately determines how you feel.[lxxv]

The next time you assume that someone has "made" you feel something, try removing them from the equation entirely. Shift the focus back to yourself. Identify the feeling and then use your coping skills to work through it.

DEALING WITH FEARS OF ABANDONMENT

Do you constantly worry that people will reject or abandon you? Perhaps you cut people off before they can reject you.

Maybe you find yourself acting clingy—calling them several times per day, sending them lots of messages, feeling desperate when they go out without you, or threatening self-harm if they end the relationship.

Abandonment fears have two underlying causes. The first is a lack of self-esteem. The second is a lack of object constancy.

BUILDING SELF-ESTEEM

If you dislike yourself, it's hard to imagine that anyone else could accept you. This attitude will get in the way of building healthy relationships.

To build your self-esteem, you need to:

- Accept your past and overcome unhealthy shame
- Learn to soothe yourself and regulate your own feelings, which in turn will help you make better decisions
- Learn to see your life and situation realistically by identifying and correcting your thinking errors
- Improve your communication skills and learn how to relate better to others

If you think these points sound familiar, it's because we've already addressed them. The self-help techniques in this book will all make a big difference if you practice them regularly. Keeping a job or volunteering can also boost your self-esteem. The tips in the next chapter will help you work with others.

OBJECT CONSTANCY

The second cause of abandonment fears is a lack of object constancy. Object constancy is the ability to understand that something—including a person or relationship—still exists even when you can't see, hear, or feel it.

Of course, on an intellectual level, people with BPD know that the other person still exists when they are away. But some psychologists believe that people with BPD don't accept this on an emotional, intuitive level. They don't see people as whole beings but as figures that are "all good" or "all bad," "gone" or "here." This is why separation frightens them and, in some cases, triggers extreme behaviors like threatening to commit suicide if a partner ends a relationship.[lxxvi] They aren't manipulative; they are genuinely terrified at the thought of abandonment.

Fortunately, this problem can be overcome by developing the ability to see people as whole individuals. This will allow you to appreciate that someone can be "here" and "not here" at the same time instead of casting them in the role of "bad and absent" or "good and here for me." The chapter on cognitive distortions will help you develop these skills, especially the tips on black and white thinking.

WHEN TO TELL A FRIEND OR PARTNER YOU HAVE BPD

You don't have to tell anyone else you have BPD. It's up to you to decide what you share and when. However, if your BPD symptoms are noticeable and often cause you problems, it might be a good idea to tell your loved ones. Learning you have BPD can help them understand your behaviors and communication style.

Be prepared to educate them about what BPD is. Pick out a couple of books or websites in advance. Ask your loved one whether they would like to learn more about BPD. Some people will be eager to do as much reading as possible. Others will prefer to get to know you better as a person directly. Either way, you need to respect their decision.

Some people are not willing to date or be friends with anyone with BPD or any other type of mental illness. They might believe some of the myths surrounding BPD, or they may not want to invest time and energy learning about it. Again, you need to appreciate that it's their decision to make. Don't waste your time trying to make them accept or understand you. Move on and find people who are a better fit for you.

WHEN TO GET PROFESSIONAL HELP

If you've been practicing the skills in this chapter for several weeks but aren't seeing any progress, it's time to get further help from a therapist. Group therapy can be particularly effective for learning social skills because you can practice them in a safe environment. Consider couple's counseling if you have a partner and your relationship has become toxic or unstable. People with BPD can and do marry, have children, and enjoy healthy friendships. You can join them.

SUMMARY

- Unstable relationships are a common problem for people with BPD.
- Working on your interpersonal relationship skills will help you better communicate with, and relate to, others.
- To overcome a fear of abandonment, you need to improve your self-esteem and object constancy.
- Self-help can improve your quality of life and relationships, but BPD is a complex condition with childhood

roots. You may need to get professional help if you aren't making much progress on your own.

- It's up to you to decide if and when you want to tell other people that you have BPD.
- If your relationship has fallen into a rut or a destructive communication cycle, consider getting help from a relationship therapist who has experience working with BPD.

CHAPTER 11:

HOW TO HANDLE WORK WHEN YOU HAVE BPD

W ork is a major source of stress for many people, but having BPD can make it even harder. At home, you can retreat to another room or use your favorite coping mechanism when you feel overwhelmed. But at work, you are bound by someone else's schedule and have to conduct yourself in a particular way. However, it's possible to hold down a job and build a career while living with BPD. This chapter will show you how.

Exercise: How Does Your Work Affect Your Wellbeing?

If you work, does your job trigger your BPD symptoms? If you aren't sure, keep a diary for a few days. Is there anything, or anyone, at work that seems to affect your moods? If you aren't currently working, think back to your last job, if you had one. What problems did you come up against, if any?

CAN EVERYONE WITH BPD HOLD DOWN A JOB?

Most people with BPD can work, especially if they are going through or have finished treatment. In fact, regular work can be a key part of BPD recovery. Holding a structured, stable job provides a daily and weekly routine. Earning your own money can bolster your self-esteem and independence. Building a career or performing well in your job helps you build a good self-image, meaning you will be less likely to look to other people for approval. Most therapists recommend people with BPD try to stay in work or study.

WHY IS WORKING WITH BPD SO CHALLENGING?

If you have BPD, you might find work tough because:

1. **You have to hide your emotions from colleagues or customers.**

   Concealing mood swings uses a lot of mental energy, and this can be exhausting. Knowing you are only one or two outbursts away from losing your job makes the situation even more stressful.

2. **You have to accept and act on feedback and criticism.**

   For someone with BPD, criticism can be devastating. It's normal to feel upset or disappointed if you are told that your work needs to improve, but if you have BPD, it can feel like the end of the world.

3. **You need to develop constructive relationships with others.**

   You may feel as though no one understands you or that you will always be an outsider. Lots of people think they don't fit in at work, but this can be especially challenging for someone with BPD.

4. **You may think your job is fantastic one day, then terrible the next.**

   Because people with BPD see the world from a black and white perspective, a single setback or bad day at work can convince them that the job is awful or unbearable.

   If you have BPD, you might have a long work history, changing jobs every few months. Perhaps you begin every new job with a sense of great hope and excitement, and feel very sad, empty, or disappointed when you come up against a challenge at work. You might initially like your boss and co-workers, perhaps even idealizing them.

   Then, when they inevitably give you some criticism or feedback, you find it hard to cope, reacting with anger, shame, or deep sadness. Because you tend to experience any form of criticism as rejection, it is difficult for you to believe that other people like you unless they are constantly positive about your work and receptive to all your ideas.

   Exercise: Spotting Patterns In Your Work History

   Write down a list of all the jobs or voluntary positions you've ever held. How long did you stay in each job? How did your feelings about the job change over time? Looking over your work history, do you identify with the pattern of job-hopping described above?

5. **You may find it hard to fit treatment, such as therapy, around your working week.**

   BPD treatment often lasts for months or years. Finding the time to attend therapy or a part-time outpatient program isn't easy if you work full-time. Depending on the kind of job and colleagues you have, you might worry about keeping your treatment a secret.

6. **Your preferences and ambitions might change frequently.**

   If your sense of self and identity changes a lot, you will have problems settling on a career path or setting goals for yourself. Some days you may feel your current job suits you well; other times, you might become obsessed with the possibility of retraining in a totally new field. Everyone wonders what it would be like to pursue other careers, but people with BPD are more likely to act on impulse, changing their plans on a whim.

7. **Under stress, your symptoms might get worse.**

   For example, if you tend to feel paranoid when under pressure, you may become convinced that your co-workers or customers dislike you, which can be frightening and upsetting. If you dissociate or "zone out" when overwhelmed, getting through your to-do list and remaining productive can feel impossible.

8. **You might have other mental health conditions, such as depression, that affect your work.**

   Most people with BPD also have at least one other psychiatric diagnosis, and therefore have to deal with lots of difficult symptoms at work. For example, if you also have depression, finding the motivation to complete projects will be tough. If you have social anxiety, interacting with co-workers will stress you out.

9. **There is still considerable stigma attached to mental illness, and few people understand BPD.**
This can cause a range of problems. For example, if your colleagues make jokes or dismissive remarks about people with mental illness, this can be upsetting. Deciding if and when to tell people about your BPD can be a minefield.

GETTING ALONG WITH YOUR COLLEAGUES

Earlier in this book, we looked at strategies for building and keeping healthy relationships. Most of these skills are just as useful at work as they are with friends and relatives. The principles are the same. Let's recap:

- Take responsibility for your own feelings
- Learn to avoid telling stories on other people
- Know how and when to listen
- Be ready to give a sincere apology if you hurt someone
- Practice saying "no"
- Know when to compromise
- Know when to take a break when the conversation gets heated

Be careful when socializing with people at work, for example, at a company reception or social event. Even in a friendly workplace, it's best to stay professional. If you tend to overshare details about your life with people you don't know very well, pay close attention to what you are saying and how you say it. Follow your colleagues' lead. If they tend to stick to superficial, light chitchat, do likewise.

Here are a few more tips to keep your workplace relationships running smoothly:

1. **If you tend to be impulsive, give yourself some breathing space when you need to make an important decision.**

   Your first instinct may be correct, but it's best to sit on a problem for a while before committing yourself to a solution. When you have to send an email or message about a sensitive topic, wait a few minutes, and reread it a few times before hitting "send."

2. **Give your co-workers the benefit of the doubt, especially if they are busy or stressed.**

   In an ideal world, we would always be polite to our colleagues. In reality, we all snap occasionally and have a bad day. Unless your colleagues are consistently unkind or rude, try to assume that their feelings or remarks aren't about you.

Exercise: Taking A Different Perspective

Imagine that you meet a colleague one morning in the hallway. Instead of saying "Hi" or "Good morning," they ignore you and go straight to the break room. There's a small chance they are mad at you, but there are lots of other possible explanations. What might they be? Thinking of alternative explanations will prevent you from getting upset over other people's behavior that has nothing to do with you.

3. **Don't expect to make friends with everyone at work.**

   Unless you run your own business, you cannot choose your colleagues. For most people, making friends at work is a bonus, not an expectation. Not everyone will want to be your friend, and that's OK. Some people with BPD find this hard to accept, particularly if they long for approval and close friendships.

4. **Think carefully before talking to your boss or colleagues about your mental health.**
In many countries, it is illegal to discriminate against an employee on the basis of mental illness. Unfortunately, the reality is that some bosses and HR staff are wary of hiring people with mental health problems.

Every workplace and job is slightly different, so it is impossible to give advice that will work for everyone. You will need to use your best judgment in deciding whether to disclose the fact that you have a mental health problem and how much detail you want to provide.

5. **Don't say anything about a colleague you wouldn't want them to overhear.**
It's tempting to vent about an annoying colleague, but resist the urge to talk negatively about others behind their backs or to spread gossip. You never know who is friends with whom, or who could be listening in. Talk about your frustrations with a loved one or therapist instead.

6. **Don't put yourself down or speak poorly of your own abilities.**
Some people with BPD make a lot of self-deprecating remarks because they believe themselves to be incom-

petent, or because they don't want to appear arrogant. Unfortunately, this strategy only makes their colleagues uneasy. No one wants to work with someone who isn't capable of doing their job, and neither do they want to play the role of therapist to a co-worker.

HANDLING CRITICISM

No one enjoys receiving criticism, but it's a normal part of working life. Feedback helps us understand where we've gone wrong and how we can improve in the future. Everyone, even the best performers, has to accept criticism at times.

As a person with BPD, you are probably more sensitive to criticism than other people. Here's how to deal with it:

1. **If you receive verbal criticism, summarize the other person's points in your own words.**
   Check to see whether you've understood what the other person has said before responding.

2. **Separate your self-worth from your performance at work.**
   This is a big challenge for most people, but if you can do it, you'll find it much easier to take criticism. Take a broader perspective. Criticism doesn't detract from your good qualities, and it doesn't determine your worth as a person. Neither does it cancel out everything you've done well in the past. There's truth in the cliché that we are all more than our jobs. Try to focus not on what criticism says about you as a person, but how you can do better in the future.

3. **Ask how you can improve.**

   Write up the other person's instructions and suggestions as notes. Knowing what you need to change will help you feel in control of the situation. Work with your supervisor to set goals.

4. **Take the opportunity to show that you are calm and professional when under pressure.**

   If you react badly to criticism—lashing out or becoming defensive, for instance—your reputation will suffer. By staying composed and concentrating on what you can do to address the problem, you will impress your supervisors and co-workers.

5. **Remember that not everyone is very good at giving feedback.**

   Some managers receive little or no training in how to share constructive criticism. This doesn't excuse managers who resort to bullying or intimidation, but it does mean you shouldn't take their incompetence personally. For example, some people do not appreciate the importance of concrete feedback and improvement plans, so their criticism isn't particularly helpful.

KNOWING WHEN TO QUIT YOUR JOB

Job-hopping is a common pattern for people with BPD, and you might have done it yourself. However, sometimes leaving a job is a smart move. The question is, how do you know whether your urge to quit is based on sound reasoning or a passing impulse?

The first thing to consider is whether you are safe at work. If you are at risk of harm, then it's best to quit if you can't work with management to solve the problem. Next, if you aren't in immediate danger, ask yourself whether something specific has triggered your urge to resign. Has a particular person or situation made you angry or upset? Are you using any thinking errors? Is your reaction in proportion to the trigger?

Give yourself at least a week to make your decision. Talk to a trusted friend, relative, therapist, or someone else outside of work. They cannot and should not tell you what to do, but talking your problem through can help you come to a decision. Making a pros and cons list of factors related to leaving versus staying in your job can also be useful.

Unless you're in an unsafe or abusive work environment, try to stay in your job until you have a new position lined up.

SELF-EMPLOYMENT AND BPD

For people who find it hard or impossible to form good relationships at work or stick to their boss' schedule, self-employment could be a tempting option. In some cases, it's a great solution. Self-employed people can choose how to run their businesses and who to work for, and they can pick their working hours. This makes it easier to fit therapy and other commitments into the week.

Note that almost all jobs, even those done remotely, still require some communication skills. For example, if you decide to work as a freelance designer or writer, you will still have to discuss projects with clients via email, video call, or an in-person meeting. You'll also need to be highly organized and self-motivated.

SUMMARY

- Lots of people with BPD can hold down a job, and there is evidence that working a stable job is good for mental health.
- Drawing on the communication skills you learned earlier in this book will help you build strong working relationships.
- Learning to take criticism is a key skill that will help improve your performance.
- Before leaving your job, talk it over with someone you can trust to give you a balanced view. Unless you are in danger, never quit on impulse. Give yourself at least a week to weigh your options, and try to get another job lined up before you resign.
- Self-employment suits some, but not all, people with BPD.

CHAPTER 12:

HOW TO COPE WITH SELF-INJURY & SUICIDAL BEHAVIORS

In this chapter, we'll look at how to cope when you have an urge to self-harm and how to deal with suicidal thoughts.

Warning: This chapter mentions methods people use to harm themselves. If you are feeling emotionally vulnerable or unsafe right now, it may be best to read this chapter another time or to read it with someone you trust.

WHAT DOES "SELF-HARM" MEAN?

Media stereotypes of people who self-harm usually show young women who cut themselves, but anyone can do it. Some people hit, bite, pinch, scratch, or burn themselves. Others may overdose, exercise excessively, deprive themselves of sleep, starve themselves, or deliberately seek out physical fights they cannot win.

Why Do People With BPD Harm Themselves?

Everyone's experience is different, but here are some reasons:

BPD is a chronic condition. You might have been suffering for years, and the thought of continuing to live with extreme mood swings and other symptoms may be too much to bear. If you have tried and failed to get help, you might feel powerless against your illness.

BPD often comes with other mental illnesses. If you have other psychiatric conditions, such as depression, they might also make you more vulnerable to self-harm and suicidal behavior.

Impulsivity is common in BPD. If you are impulsive, you are more likely than most people to act on sudden destructive urges. Drinking and taking drugs can make impulsivity worse.

Some people use self-harm as a means of translating emotional pain into physical pain, dealing with difficult memories, or as a way of distracting themselves from their problems. Others use it as a form of punishment. People who dissociate may use self-harm as a way to ground themselves. It's possible to become dependent on self-harming as a coping mechanism. It can take weeks or months to stop.

You may hear some people talk about self-harm as a manipulative or attention-seeking behavior. This is an unhelpful, judgmental stance for two reasons. First, most people keep their self-harm a secret. Second, self-harming for attention is a sign that something is seriously wrong and that the person needs help.

The mental health charity Mind suggests there are three ways you can reduce your urge to self-harm: identifying your triggers, using distraction techniques, and delaying the urge.[lxxvii]

FIND YOUR TRIGGERS

Learning more about your self-harm helps you regain control. Start keeping a notebook. Every time you self-harm, write down what you were doing and thinking beforehand. Do particular feelings, situations, people, anniversaries, music, or even times of the day trigger you?

TUNE INTO YOUR BODY

Identify the warning signs. How does your body feel when you want to self-harm? Do you feel warm, shivery, heavy, or dissociated? Do you have thoughts like, "I'm going to do it"? Write them down in your notebook.

FIND DISTRACTIONS THAT WORK FOR YOU

The next step is to practice using distractions when you notice your personal warning signs.

Try:

- Ripping up paper, punching a cushion, shouting, running, or dancing energetically if you feel angry.
- Giving yourself a massage, listening to relaxing music, petting an animal, taking a bath, or taking a rest if you feel afraid or sad.
- Make a to-do list, draw up a schedule, write a letter expressing your feelings, or tidy up your living space if you feel overwhelmed.
- Have a cold shower, flick a rubber band against your wrist, squeeze some ice cubes, or smell something with a strong odor if you feel numb or spaced out.

- Do some vigorous exercise, challenge negative thoughts about yourself, remind yourself of your good qualities, and remind yourself that no one is perfect if you feel ashamed.

Try Delaying Self-Harm

If you still feel compelled to self-harm, wait five minutes first. If you can, wait another five minutes, and so on. You may find that the urge goes away altogether. If it doesn't and you do end up self-harming, don't feel guilty. Self-harm can take on an addictive quality. You might need to work with a therapist to get it under control.

Coping With Suicidal Thoughts

Thinking about suicide does not necessarily mean you want to die. It's a sign that you can't cope with your current problems and can't imagine a better future. Feeling suicidal does not mean you are weak or that your BPD is too severe for treatment. It simply means that you are in a great deal of pain.

Here's what to do in a time of crisis:

- Promise yourself that you won't act on your plans until you've tried to get help.
- Talk to someone as soon as possible. This could be your doctor, a crisis line, or a loved one. If someone doesn't answer the phone, call someone else.
- Get yourself into a safe place away from anything you could use to harm yourself.
- Call for an ambulance if you don't feel safe.
- Refrain from drugs and alcohol because they can impair your judgment.

- Remind yourself that all feelings pass eventually.
- If you can, use your favorite coping strategies from this book, such as grounding exercises and music therapy.

Above all, take your thoughts and feelings seriously.

DRAWING UP A CRISIS PLAN

When you are struggling with suicidal thoughts, having a crisis plan in place can be reassuring. Your plan should outline the coping strategies you will try when you have suicidal thoughts, along with the phone numbers of crisis lines, loved ones, and any mental health professionals involved in your care. Keep a copy with you at all times. If you are getting treatment from a doctor or therapist, ask them to help you draw up a plan.

SUMMARY

- Self-harm is common among people with BPD.
- Most people self-harm as a way of expressing or coping with intense emotional pain.
- It's possible to become dependent on self-harm, and it can be hard to quit.
- Short and long-term coping strategies include distraction, delay, and emotional regulation skills.
- Thinking about suicide does not necessarily mean you want to die, or that you will make an attempt on your life.
- No matter how severe your pain or the scale of your problems, there is hope.
- Creating a crisis plan will help keep you safe. Keep a copy with you at all times and share it with people you trust.

CHAPTER 13:

HOW TO SUPPORT SOMEONE WITH BPD

Perhaps you picked up this book not because you have BPD, but because you know someone who does. If so, this chapter was written especially for you. Being a friend, partner, relative, or colleague of a person with BPD presents special challenges. At times, you may be confused or hurt by their behavior.

If you've read this book through from the beginning, you already understand what BPD is and how it's treated. You've taken perhaps the most important step of all—educating yourself.

FOCUS ON THE INDIVIDUAL, NOT THEIR DISORDER

BPD is a serious disorder, but people with BPD are much more than their symptoms. Moreover, not all people with BPD are alike. Never assume that you are more of an expert on BPD than your loved one. Ask them what they wish other people understood about BPD, what challenges they face, and how you can support them.

Keep an open mind. Some people are excellent at hiding their difficulties, and some of the problems associated with BPD are invisible. For example, your loved one might struggle with frequent feelings of depression or be very concerned with earning your approval. Just like any other friendship or relationship, you will come to understand more about their personality and problems as you grow closer.

ARE YOU SOMEONE'S "FAVORITE PERSON"?

If you've read blogs and articles online about BPD, you might have come across the term "favorite person" or FP. An FP is someone a person with BPD feels they cannot live without.

Your loved one might not tell you that you're their FP, but if they seem emotionally reliant on you, there's a good chance they have cast you in this role.

According to BPD expert and researcher John Gunderson, people with BPD are on a mission—whether they realize it or not—to find a person that will make them feel unconditionally loved, safe, and accepted. They are searching for the attachment figure they didn't get as young children.

Because the person with BPD is looking for unconditional support and love, they are bound to be disappointed, because no human being can provide what they are looking for. This can start a vicious cycle: they desperately seek intimacy from their FP but drive the FP away with their neediness. This causes them to cling on even tighter. Eventually, the FP may be forced to cut loose and end the relationship, which traumatizes the person with BPD and leaves them feeling rejected and unlovable.

Here are some guidelines for anyone who lives, loves, or works with someone with BPD. If you are an FP, these rules are even more essential.

1. **Encourage them to build a wide support network, including professional helpers.**
   No one can be, or should be, another person's only source of emotional support. You can't force someone to make new friends or reach out for help, but you can gently suggest that they try to meet new people.

2. **Feel free to talk about other people in your life.**
   Don't be afraid to talk about your other friendships and family relationships. If you are an FP, it's tempting to indulge your loved one's fantasies that they are the only person you think and care about. Resist that urge. You need to make it clear that while you value them and their company, you are not dependent on their affection or approval.

3. **Talk on the phone or face to face rather than over text.**
   It's hard to capture tone and nuance in text messages. Have conversations in person or on the phone if possible, especially if you need to talk about a sensitive issue. People with BPD are good at overanalyzing brief messages and jumping to conclusions.

4. **Don't offer continual reassurance.**
   It isn't your job to keep your loved one happy. It's reasonable to offer them occasional reassurance that you love or like them, but they are responsible for managing their own feelings, however uncomfortable that may be.

5. **Remind your loved one of their strengths.**
   If your loved one has low self-esteem and a shaky identity, they will lose sight of their talents and positive traits.

Bolster their self-image by paying them sincere compliments when you get a chance.

6. **Encourage your loved one to form their own ideas and opinions.**

   People with BPD are often keen to impress their favorite people, and some will go to extraordinary lengths to do so. In extreme cases, they will start dressing like their FP, adopt the same opinions, and even start copying their tone of voice, posture, and sense of humor. If you think your loved one is mimicking you, gently encourage them to focus on what they like and enjoy outside of your relationship.

7. **Be honest about what you can offer.**

   This is a good rule for any relationship, but it's particularly important if the other person has BPD. Setting clear expectations up front will save both of you a lot of pain later. For example, suppose you have a friend with BPD who has started to flirt with you. As flattering as this kind of attention may be, it's best to shut it down quickly and draw firm boundaries if you don't want to get into a romantic or sexual relationship.

8. **Set boundaries.**

   For example, if your loved one tends to call late at night to talk about their problems, you can set a "No calling after 9 p.m." boundary. If they get angry easily, you won't be able to control their temper, but you can set a firm boundary around toxic or abusive behaviors such as name-calling.

   It's common for people with BPD to idealize an FP one moment, then devalue them the next after a minor argument. However, you do not have to tolerate being disrespected. You are not an emotional punching bag.

9. **Don't take ultimate responsibility for their feelings.**

You have an obligation to be respectful and compassionate towards your loved one, but you are not their therapist or doctor. If they blame you for a mistake or error of judgment, you don't have to accept their opinion as fact. You cannot "fix" someone else; you will only grow tired and resentful if you try.

10. **Prepare for the unexpected.**

You can't control someone else's thoughts or behaviors, but you can prepare yourself so the ups and downs of the relationship don't take a toll on your own mental health. For example, it's reasonable to expect a friend with BPD to be much happier or angrier some days than others for no clear reason.

11. **Do not stay in a relationship or be friends with someone because you feel sorry for them.**

Both you and the other person have a right to enjoy mutually beneficial relationships, and relationships based on a sense of duty or pity don't fit this definition.

12. **Work on your communication skills together.**

Earlier in the book, we looked at how good communication is the foundation of all good relationships. Talk to your loved one about how you can work as a team to improve your skills. Suggest that you read through the chapter together and practice the exercises. When you can share your thoughts and feelings without fear of the other person's reactions, you'll have fewer misunderstandings.

TAKING CARE OF YOURSELF

Watching someone you care about struggle with their mental health is painful, especially if you see them every day. You might feel frustrated, sad, or even angry if their behavior is challenging.

Look out for your own welfare. You deserve time to pursue your own interests and hobbies, to have time and space to yourself, and to nurture your mental health. Stay in touch with your family and friends. It's natural to support your loved one, but don't make them the center of your universe. Set personal and professional goals, make your work or study a priority, and build a well-rounded life.[lxxviii]

Find healthy outlets for your emotions. Some people find journaling helps. Others go to the gym, spend time in nature, or throw themselves into creative projects. Talking to other people can be a good way to vent, but be careful if you take part in an online community. Remember that no one online can offer you expert advice. Forums and message boards can also become toxic places if members use the space to continually complain about their partners instead of seeking constructive support.

It's possible to have a happy long-term relationship with someone diagnosed with BPD, but visiting a couple's therapist is a smart move if you keep arguing. Make sure your therapist has experience treating people with BPD.

BPD AND ABUSE

Most people with BPD are not abusive, but those who have particular trouble controlling their emotions can be aggressive to themselves and others.[lxxix] For example, they may find it difficult to control their anger during an argument and lash out physically or verbally.

People with BPD did not ask to develop their condition, and they deserve compassion. At the same time, it is their responsibility to seek help and change their behavior if and when it hurts others. If your loved one is abusive but expects you to forgive them because they have BPD, they are not showing you the respect you deserve.

Ultimately, if your loved one shows no desire to change, you need to assess whether you want to continue the relationship. It doesn't matter whether or not they have a psychiatric condition—no one, including you, should be expected to stay with an abuser.

SUPPORTING SOMEONE WHO SELF-HARMS

Discovering that someone close to you has injured themself can be shocking, but try not to overreact. If you appear upset or angry, your loved one will be less likely to confide in you in the future. Validate their emotions. Never minimize their fears or feelings. Even if you think their problems are trivial, respect their personal experience.

People who self-harm are in considerable emotional pain, and injuring themselves is a coping mechanism. In general, self-harm isn't done for attention. However, even if your loved one has deliberately harmed themself in the hope of making people understand their pain, they deserve compassion. Someone in deep distress can't always tell others directly what they want or need.

Do not assume that someone who self-harms wants to commit suicide. Most people who self-harm don't hope to end their lives; they are trying to manage overwhelming thoughts and feelings. Don't try to force change by telling them to "just stop." People with BPD need to build up healthier coping skills, and they often need to work through their problems with a therapist, and this can take time. Be patient and supportive.

WHAT TO DO WHEN SOMEONE SAYS THEY WANT TO END THEIR OWN LIFE

Suicidal thoughts can be short-lived or long-lasting, subtle or intense. They can change quickly. Some people feel more comfortable than others about sharing how they feel. If your loved one feels suicidal, they may not let you know.

It's not always clear when someone feels suicidal. Some warning signs are subtle. They include sadness, moodiness, giving away valued possessions, social withdrawal, changes in personality or appearance, and suddenly appearing calmer or more at peace than usual. Never blame yourself for not seeing the signs. Even mental health professionals sometimes miss them.

1. **Take suicide threats seriously.**

   Suicidal behavior should never be dismissed as "attention-seeking," even if the person has made threats before without following through. Listen to your loved one and validate their feelings.

2. **Do not leave the person alone if possible.**

3. **Hide any objects or medication that someone could use to hurt themselves.**

4. **Ask your loved one if they have a crisis plan in place.**

   They may have already put a plan together to deal with suicidal thoughts. This plan may include coping strategies and people to call. Help them work through the plan.

5. **Call for professional help.**

   If your loved one is in immediate danger, call an ambulance. A mental health professional is best placed to decide whether your loved one is at serious risk of harming themselves.

SUMMARY

- You will need to set firm boundaries, build your communication skills, and learn to respect your own needs if you hope to have a happy relationship with someone who has BPD.
- Encourage your loved one to build out their social circle and become more independent.
- You don't have to stay with someone who abuses you, even if they have been diagnosed with a mental illness.
- If your loved one self-harms, try to remain supportive and non-judgmental.
- If someone threatens suicide or shows any other signs of suicidal behavior, always take the situation seriously.

CONCLUSION

You've reached the end of this guide to BPD. You can now say confidently that you know what BPD is, what treatments are available, and how to live a satisfying life as you learn how to deal with your symptoms. Having learned about attachment theory and the latest research into the biology of BPD, you now understand why some of us are more likely than others to develop this condition.

Armed with this knowledge, you can start putting together a plan for taking back control and looking toward a brighter future. Many people with BPD benefit from professional help, but self-help will give you a head start. The more you know about BPD and the more coping strategies you learn, the better. Even if you receive a different diagnosis, the skills you've picked up in this book help everyone, not just those with BPD, develop their emotional intelligence.

If you don't have BPD but know someone who does, thank you for taking the time to learn about it. In doing so, you'll be able to offer support to those with this condition. In a world where myths about mental illness still hold people back from getting the help they need, your compassion and understanding is a gift.

BPD is a complex and challenging disorder, but there is hope. Every day, people with BPD learn to cope with their emotions, build healthy friendships, and thrive in romantic relationships. If you have BPD, please know that you are worthy of love, acceptance, and help. You fully deserve the best life has to offer. With the right support, you can get it.

THANKS FOR READING!

I really hope you enjoyed this book and, most of all, got more value from it than you had to give.

It would mean a lot to me if you left an Amazon review—I will reply to all questions asked!

Please visit www.pristinepublish.com/bpdreview to leave a review.

Be sure to check out my email list, where I am constantly adding tons of value. The best way to get on the list currently is by visiting www.pristinepublish.com/empathbonus and entering your email.

Here I'll provide actionable information that aims to improve your enjoyment of life. I'll update you on my latest books, and I'll even send free e-books that I think you'll find useful.

Kindest regards,

Judy Dyer

REFERENCES

i   Kivi, R., & Leonard, M. (2016). *Borderline Personality Disorder*

ii NHS. (n.d.). *Borderline personality disorder*

iii MIND. (2020). *Personality disorders.*

iv Salters-Pedneault, K. (2019). *Borderline Personality Disorder (BPD) Criteria for Diagnosis.*

v   Korzekwa, M.I., Dell, P.F., Links, P.S., Thabane, L., & Fougere, P. (2009). Dissociation in borderline personality disorder: a detailed look. *Journal of Trauma and Dissociation.*

vi Ekeberg, O., Kvarstein, E.H., Urnes, O., Ulltveit-Moe Eikenæs, I., & Hem, E. (2019). Suicidal patients with personality disorder. Tidsskr Nor Legeforen.

vii Gunderson, J.G. (2011). Borderline Personality Disorder. *The New England Journal of Medicine.*

viii Juurlink, T.T., Vukadin, M., Stringer, B., Westerman, M.J., Lamers, F., Anema, J.R., Beekman, A.T.F., & van Marle, H.J.F. (2019). Barriers and facilitators to employment in borderline personality disorder: A qualitative study among patients, mental health practitioners and insurance physicians.

ix Gross, R., Olfson, M., & Gameroff, M. (2002). Borderline Personality Disorder in Primary Care. Archives of Internal Medicine.

x   Adler, K.A., Finch, E.F., Rodriguez-Villa, A.M., & Choi-Kain, L.W. (2019). *Primary Care Providers.* In L.W. Choi-Kain & J.G. Gunderson (Eds.)., *Applications of Good Psychiatric Management for Borderline Personality Disorder: A Practical Guide.*

xi Hawkins, A.A., Furr, R.M., Mayfield Arnold, E., Law, M.K., Mniemne, M., & Fleeson, W. (2014). The Structure of Borderline Personality Disorder Symptoms: A Multi-method, Multi-sample Examination. *Personality Disorders.*

[xii] Knott, L. (2016). Emotionally Unstable Personality Disorder.

[xiii] Lo, I. (2019). Do You Have "Quiet BPD"?

[xiv] Chun, S., Harris, A., & Bornovalova, A. (2017). A psychometric investigation of gender differences and common processes across Borderline and Antisocial Personality Disorders. *Journal of Abnormal Psychology.*

[xv] Stepp, S.D., & Pilkonis, P.A. (2008). Age-Related Differences in Individual DSM Criteria for Borderline Personality Disorder. *Journal of Personality Disorders.*

[xvi] Biskin, R.S., & Paris, J. (2012). Diagnosing borderline personality disorder. *Canadian Medical Association Journal.*

[xvii] Zanarini, M.C., Frankenburg, F.R., Reich, B., & Fitzmaurice, G. (2012). Attainment and Stability of Sustained Symptomatic Remission and Recovery Among Patients With Borderline Personality Disorder and Axis II Comparison Subjects: A 16-Year Prospective Follow-Up Study. *The American Journal of Psychiatry.*

[xviii] Coid, J.W., Ullrich, S., Kallis. C., et al. (2016). Improving risk management for violence in mental health services: a multimethods approach. NIHR Journals Library.

[xix] Gunderson, John & Herpertz, Sabine & E. Skodol, Andrew & Torgersen, Svenn & C. Zanarini, Mary. (2018). Borderline personality disorder. *Nature Reviews Disease Primers.*

[xx] National Institute of Mental Health. (2017). *Borderline Personality Disorder.*

[xxi] Skodol, A. (2019). *Borderline Personality Disorder (BPD).*

[xxii] Malek, M., William, F., Mayfield, E.A., & Michael, F.R. (2018). Differentiating the everyday emotion dynamics of borderline personality disorder from major depressive disorder and bipolar disorder. *Personality Disorders: Theory, Research, and Treatment.*

[xxiii] Barnhill, J.W. (2018). *Posttraumatic Stress Disorder (PTSD).*

[xxiv] National Educational Alliance for Borderline Personality Disorder. (2020). *Making The Diagnosis.*

[xxv] Biskin, R.S., & Paris, J. (2013). Comorbidities in Borderline Personality Disorder. Psychiatric Times.

[xxvi] Skoglund, C., Tiger, A., Ruck, C., Petrovic, P., Asherton, P., Hellner, C., Mataix-Cols, D., & Kuja-Halkola, R. (2019). Familial risk and heritability of diagnosed borderline personality disorder: A register study of the Swedish population. Molecular Psychiatry.

[xxvii] Torgersen, S., Lygren, S., Oien, P.A., Skre, I., Onstad, S., Edvardsen, J., Tambs, K., & Kringlen, E. (2000). A twin study of personality disorders. *Comprehensive Psychiatry.*

[xxviii] Stepp, S.D., Whalen, D.J., Scott, L.N., Zalewski, M., Loeber, R., & Hipwell, A.E. (2014). Reciprocal-effects of parenting and borderline personality disorder symptoms in adolescent girls. *Developmental Psychopathology.*

[xxix] Koenigsberg, H.W., & Siever, L.J. (2000). The Frustrating No-Man's-Land of Borderline Personality Disorder.

[xxx] Lischke, A., Herpertz, S.C., Berger, C., Domes, G., & Gamer, M. (2017). Divergent effects of oxytocin on (para-)limbic reactivity to emotional and neutral scenes in females with and without borderline personality disorder. *Social Cognitive and Affective Neuroscience.*

[xxxi] Crowell, S.E., Beauchaine, T.P., & Linehan, M.M. (2009). A Biosocial Developmental Model of Borderline Personality: Elaborating and Extending Linehan's Theory. *Psychological Bulletin.*

[xxxii] Salters-Pedneault, K. (2020). Why People With BPD Have Trouble Identifying Emotions.

[xxxiii] Gans, S. (2019). The Different Types of Attachment Styles.

[xxxiv] Bateman, A., & Fonagy, P. (2010). Mentalization based treatment for borderline personality disorder. *World Psychiatry.*

[xxxv] Bakermans-Kranenburg, M., & van Ijzendoorn, M.H. (2009). The first 10,000 Adult Attachment Interviews: Distributions of adult attachment representations in clinical and non-clinical groups. *Attachment & Human Development.*

[xxxvi] Agrawal, H.R., Gunderson, J., Holmes, B.M., & Lyons-Ruth, K. (2004). Attachment Studies with Borderline Patients: A Review. *Harvard Review of Psychiatry.*

[xxxvii] Silk, K.R., Wolf, T.L., Ben-Ami, D.A., & Poortinga, E.W. (2005). Environmental Factors in the Etiology of Borderline Personality Disorder. In M.C. Zanarini (Ed.), *Borderline Personality Disorder.*

xxxviii Krause-Utz, A., Erol, E., Brousianou, A.V., Cackowski, S., Paret, C., Ende, G., & Elzinga, B. (2019). Self-reported impulsivity in women with borderline personality disorder: the role of childhood maltreatment severity and emotion regulation difficulties. *Borderline Personality Disorder and Emotion Dysregulation.*

xxxix Kuo, J.R., Khoury, J.E., Metcalfe, R., Fitzpatrick, S., & Goodwill, A. (2015). An examination of the relationship between childhood emotional abuse and borderline personality disorder features: The role of difficulties with emotion regulation. *Child Abuse & Neglect.*

xl Wolke, D., Schreier, A., Zanarini, M.C., & Winsper, C. (2012). Bullied by peers in childhood and borderline personality symptoms at 11 years of age: A prospective study. *The Journal of Child Psychology and Psychiatry.*

xli Sansone, R.A., Lam, C., & Wiederman, M.W. (2010). Being bullied in childhood: correlations with borderline personality in adulthood. *Comprehensive Psychiatry.*

xlii Tusiani-Eng, P., & Yeomans, F. (2018). Borderline Personality Disorder: Barriers to Borderline Personality Disorder Treatment and Opportunities for Advocacy. *Psychiatric Clinics of North America.*

xliii Grohol, J.M. (2019). An Overview of Dialectical Behavior Therapy.

xliv Bateman, A., & Fonagy, P. (2010). Mentalization based treatment for borderline personality disorder. *World Psychiatry.*

xlv Hoermann, S., Zupanick, C.E., & Dombeck, M. (n.d.). Transference Focused Psychotherapy For Personality Disorders.

xlvi Gunderson, J., Masland, S., & Choi-Kain, L. (2018). Good psychiatric management: a review. *Current Opinion in Psychology.*

xlvii Tusiani-Eng, P., & Yeomans, F. (2018). Borderline Personality Disorder: Barriers to Borderline Personality Disorder Treatment and Opportunities for Advocacy. *Psychiatric Clinics of North America.*

xlviii Bozzatello, P., Rocca, P., De Rosa, M.L., & Bellino, S. (2019). Current and emerging medications for borderline personality disorder: is pharmacotherapy alone enough? Expert Opinion on Pharmacotherapy.

xlix Ibid.

[l] Vollm, B., Stoffers-Winterling, J., Mattivi, J., Simonson, E., Storebo, O.J., Nielsen, S., Kielsholm, M.L., & Lieb, K. (2017). Do mood stabilizers help in borderline personality disorder. *European Psychiatry*.

[li] Salters-Pedneault, K. (2019). *Borderline Personality Disorder and Emotion Regulation*.

[lii] Salters-Pedneault, K. (2019). Anxiety Medications for Borderline Personality Disorder.

[liii] Christiansen, E., Agerbo, E., Bilenberg, N., & Stenager, E. (2016). SSRIs and risk of suicide attempts in younger people—A Danish observational register-based historical cohort study, using propensity score. *Nordic Journal of Psychiatry*.

[liv] Lavey, R., Sherman, T., Mueser, K. T., Osborne, D. D., Currier, M., & Wolfe, R. (2005). The effects of yoga on mood in psychiatric inpatients. Psychiatric Rehabilitation Journal.

[lv] Mayo Clinic. (n.d.). Massage: Get in touch with its many benefits.

[lvi] Ozkaraman, A., Dugum, O., Yilmaz, H.O., & Yesilbalkan, O.U. (2018). The effect of lavender on anxiety and sleep quality in patients treated with chemotherapy. *Clinical Journal of Oncology Nursing*.

[lvii] Hjalmarsdottir, F. (2018). 17 Science-Based Benefits of Omega-3 Fatty Acids.

[lviii] Poldinger, W. (1994). History of St. John's Wort. *Praxis*.

[lix] WebMD. (n.d.). St. John's Wort.

[lx] Fink, C. (2012). Depression: Have You Had Your Folate (Folic Acid) Levels Checked?

[lxi] Gronli, O., Kvamme, J.M., Friborg, O., & Wynn, R. (2013). Zinc Deficiency Is Common in Several Psychiatric Disorders.

[lxii] Nakamura, M., Miura, A., Nagahata, T., Shibata, Y., Okada, E., & Ojima, T. (2019). Low Zinc, Copper, and Manganese Intake is Associated with Depression and Anxiety Symptoms in the Japanese Working Population: Findings From the Eating Habit and Well-Being Study. *Nutrients*.

[lxiii] Salters-Pedneault, K. (2019). Borderline Personality Disorder and Emotion Regulation.

lxiv Schenck, L.K. (n.d.). How to Calm Down from Extreme Emotions in 30 Seconds.

lxv Salters-Pedneault, K. (2019). How Borderline Personality Disorder Can Distort Thinking Processes.

lxvi Salters-Pedneault, K. (2020). Coping With Borderline Disorder Embarrassment and Shame.

lxvii Kabat-Zinn J. (1994). Wherever you go, there you are. New York: Hyperion.

lxviii Wupperman, P., Neumann, C.S., Whitman, J.B., & Axelrod, S.R. (2009). The Role of Mindfulness in Borderline Personality Disorder Features. *The Journal of Nervous and Mental Disease.*

lxix Greater Good in Action. (n.d.). Mindful Breathing.

lxx Bertin, M. (2017). A Daily Mindful Walking Practice.

lxxi Grohol, J.M. (2019). 15 Common Cognitive Distortions.

lxxii Ibid.

lxxiii Dombeck, M. (n.d.). What Are Some Coping Skills for Paranoia?

lxxiv CS Healthcare. (n.d.). SHUSH Listening Tips – Samaritans.

lxxv Grohol, J.M. (2018). We Are Responsible for Our Own Feelings.

lxxvi Lo, I. (2018). Object Constancy: Understanding the Fear of Abandonment and Borderline Personality Disorder.

lxxvii Mind. (2016). Self-harm.

lxxviii Shushansky, L. (2017). Supporting Yourself Is A Must While Supporting Your Loved One.

lxxix Scott, L.N., Stepp, S.D., & Pilkonis, P.A. (2014). Prospective Associations Between Features of Borderline Personality Disorder, Emotion Dysregulation, and Aggression. *Personality Disorders.*

CPSIA information can be obtained at www.ICGtesting.com
Printed in the USA
BVHW032307121122
651841BV00016B/760